THE ART OF THE SAINT JOHN'S BIBLE

A Reader's Guide to

Wisdom Books and Prophets

THE ART OF THE SAINT JOHN'S BIBLE

A Reader's Guide to Wisdom Books

and Prophets BY SUSAN SINK

DONALD JACKSON – ARTISTIC DIRECTOR

THE SAINT JOHN'S BIBLE

Collegeville, Minnesota

A Saint John's Bible Book
published by
Liturgical Press

www.saintjohnsbible.org

Design by Jerry Kelly. Cover images by Donald Jackson.

ISBN 978-0-8146-9063-5

LIBRARY OF CONGRESS CATALOGING-IN-PUBLICATION DATA

Sink, Susan.
  The art of the Saint John's Bible / Susan Sink.
    p. cm.
  Includes bibliographical references and indexes.
  ISBN 978-0-8146-9062-8
  1. Saint John's Bible—Illustrations. 2. Illumination of books and manuscripts—Wales. 3. St. John's University (Collegeville, Minn.) I. Title.
  ND3355.5.S29S56 2007
  745.6'721--dc22   2007003564

The author gratefully acknowledges the contributions to this volume by several members of *The Saint John's Bible* team. I began with video recordings of Donald Jackson's presentations of *Wisdom Books* and *Prophets* to the Committee on Illumination and Text. Donald Jackson and the team in Wales also carefully read the text and offered additional information and clarifications. Both Carol Marrin and Tim Ternes generously shared stories of their experience with the text and helped me to get access to information. Again I relied primarily on Father Michael Patella, OSB, who walked me through the illuminations, read drafts, and consulted on the theological interpretations that made their way into the text. This information and these images and sacred texts are "the beginning of knowledge," and as such should never be taken as the final word.

CONTENTS

Introduction   7

Wisdom Books   11

Job Frontispiece   13
Commissioned Text Treatments   17
Out of the Whirlwind   18
The Fear of the Lord Is the Beginning of Knowledge   22
Seven Pillars of Wisdom   24
Hymn to a Virtuous Woman   26
Ecclesiastes Frontispiece   27
Garden of Desire   30
Set Me as a Seal upon Your Heart   33
Let Us Lie in Wait   35
Wisdom Woman   37
Correction   41
Creation, Covenant, Shekinah, Kingdom   42
Listen and Faithful Friends   46
Praise of Wisdom   48
Like Clay in the Hand of the Potter   50
Sirach Carpet Page   51

Prophets   53

Isaiah Reverse Carpet Page   55
Peace and Justice   57
Vision of Isaiah   58
Messianic Predictions   62
Insect Marginalia   64
Extending the Prophet's Call   66
Suffering Servant   68
Annotation   70
Arise, Shine   71
As a Mother Comforts Her Child   73
Jeremiah Frontispiece   74
Calligraphy   77
Vision at the Chebar   79
Valley of Dry Bones   82
Vision of the New Temple   86

Bless the Lord   89
Vision of the Son of Man   90
Demands of Social Justice   93
Do Justice, Love Kindness, Walk Humbly   95
Rejoice!   96

Appendices

INDEX OF VISUAL ELEMENTS   98
INDEX OF TEXT TREATMENTS   99
INDEX OF ARTISTS   105
COMMITTEE ON ILLUMINATION AND TEXT   110

INTRODUCTION

THIS SECOND VOLUME of *The Art of The Saint John's Bible* covers two important collections of literature found in the Old Testament: *Wisdom Books* and *Prophets*. Within these collections there are also multiple genres: autobiography, legend, instruction, dreams, visions, argument, and lyric love poetry. However, we are likely to know isolated pieces—a familiar proverb, for example, or a stray lyric from Handel's *Messiah*—but not be acquainted with the books as a whole. Many people know the story of Job, but few have spent any time with the actual text, considering Job's dilemma, his friends' answers, and his final dialogue with God. When we hear about Daniel we are more likely to think of his miraculous delivery from the lions' den than of the prophet's vision of the Son of Man. The long series of prophets with names like Zephaniah, Nahum, and Obadiah are sometimes seen as just one more barrier between readers and the New Testament, where Christians focus most of their attention.

When we think of the prophets we are most likely to associate them with messages of doom and a dark vision of God. The God of the Old Testament has been packaged for popular consumption as the God of fire and brimstone, a vengeful, angry figure who punishes and smites. In truth, the story here is not pretty. It is as much the story of the consequences of our inhumanity as it is a story of redemption. However, let us remember that the "inhumanity" is our responsibility, and "redemption" is where we find God. You will see this reflected in the illuminations throughout the two volumes, particularly *Prophets,* where the darker elements are balanced with the rainbow of God's everlasting promise and with the enthroned figure of God ever present to the prophets, as well as in the numerous predictions of a messiah. God is always faithful and always hopeful that the people will return to right worship and build a just society.

Wisdom Books' illuminations and text treatments further extend our vision of God. Special attention is given to passages that emphasize the feminine aspects of the divine: the nurturing, guiding, creative God. For all the time the authors of Job and Ecclesiastes spend on the problem of suffering and death, the answer that comes back is that life was made for living, and the wise person who seeks God should enjoy the splendors of creation.

The Assyrian and Babylonian invasions provide context for these books. They come out of the period when the Old Testament, even the books of the Pentateuch, were being written and assembled. During this time the region known as Canaan, the "Promised Land," which had been in the possession of the Israelites, was conquered. This was the land God had promised Abraham and delivered to Moses and Joshua. The Lord's temple was built here by Solomon in Jerusalem in the southern kingdom of Judah. The northern kingdom of Israel, the possession of ten tribes of Israel, was overthrown first by the Assyrians in the eighth century B.C.E. The southern kingdom fell in the sixth century to the Babylonians, who destroyed the temple and led the people into exile. The Old Testament was written to preserve the identity of the Israelite people, through history and *torah*, or law. It also included books that collected wisdom to be passed on from generation to generation, such as Proverbs and Wisdom, and books used in ritual celebrations, including the Song of Solomon.

What was being preserved was the identity of the people of Israel and their relationship with God. The big questions hanging over the books are these: What does it mean that we lost the land promised to us by God? Who are we, and how can we be the people of God if we have no kingdom and no temple? The prophets attempt to answer these questions as voices from before, during, and after the Exile, God's messengers to the scattered and downtrodden people seeking an explanation for what is happening to them. The prophets address the current situation of the people and also offer hope and direction for the future. The wisdom books offer practical direction for what it means to live as God's people. They encourage the people to live righteous lives even as exiles, and show them what those lives look like.

The illuminations in these books are thematic. Illuminations are never illustrations, always theological reflections. They are more than pictures accompanying the text, and in these two volumes they have the task of uniting sometimes disparate and often difficult texts. The course of the illuminations was mapped out and directed by the Committee on Illumination and Text (CIT), a team of biblical scholars, theologians, artists, and historians drawn from the Saint John's community to advise on the project. They reflected on the theological significance of these texts, the use of the texts in liturgies, and also the ways Benedictines have particularly resonated with them. Donald Jackson, the artistic director of *The Saint John's Bible,* and the CIT have never lost sight of the fact that the Bible is a living text and is meant to be used by the monastery that commissioned it as well as others. That community is comprised of the monks of Saint John's Abbey and University, who are actively engaged in practicing the Rule of Benedict as they sustain the life of the abbey, and who serve the greater community as priests, educators, musicians, artists, craftsmen, administrators, and laborers.

The themes that guide the illumination process, therefore, are also themes that guide the community. Three major themes are particularly highlighted in these volumes: hospitality, transformation, and justice for God's people. Hospitality is particularly present in the book of Wisdom, which lays out patterns for positive interaction in human communities. Transformation is dramatically seen in the illuminations depicting the visions of the prophets Ezekiel and Isaiah, although all these books call us to repent and to allow God to transform us. Justice for God's people is also a strong theme for the prophets, who are speaking to a people looking for restoration and restitution. As we have seen in *Gospels and Acts, Psalms,* and *Pentateuch,* however, attention to justice for the poor and vulnerable, for the resident aliens, widows, and orphans, continues to be God's message to the people.

The Saint John's Bible is having a dramatic impact on individuals who encounter it, whether in museum exhibits, educational programs, or in the reproduction volumes. The volumes have become a great tool for introducing people to a Benedictine practice the monks engage in daily, *lectio divina.* As directed in the Rule of Benedict, the monks spend time each day reflecting on biblical texts. They read the texts slowly and prayerfully, then focus on certain words that stand out and become the source of a deeper reflection. With *The Saint John's Bible,* educators and Benedictines associated with the project have begun using the term *visio divina* to describe the meditation practices and instruction sessions they lead. A group is invited to read the biblical text and reflect on it as they would with *lectio divina,* then to contemplate the corresponding illumination to see how the image expands their understanding of what they have been reading. Finally, they return to the text to see how the two come together. It is not unlike the Eastern Orthodox practice of reading icons. This reader's guide is designed to foster that kind of reflective experience with the text and the illuminations. It is our hope that you will spend some time with the Scripture passages and with the questions at the beginning and end of each entry that encourage you to consider the meaning behind the image. The wisdom books present the divine as nurturing and creative, where a well-kept household is a metaphor for a life in God. As a mother, God gently reprimands, but also smiles and guides us children in the way we should go. God's home is one of love, concern, and hospitality, and we are expected to act accordingly when we are in it. Be aware of the feminine imagery used throughout the illuminations of this volume. When reading the visions of the prophets, consider your own call and your own part in building God's kingdom.

As in the previous volume of the guide, this one also gives information on the composition of the illuminations and the tools used in making them. *Prophets* really marked the halfway point of the entire project. When the time came for illuminating and adding text treatments to *Wisdom Books*, all of the writing by the scribes had been completed. *Historical Books* was written, and Paul's letters, and all that remained was Revelation, which Donald Jackson had decided to write himself. This meant big changes at Donald Jackson's scriptorium in Wales, and for the five scribes, some of whom had been working on the project for six years, an end to a significant piece of work. Donald and Mabel Jackson commissioned from each of the five scribes a text treatment of his or her own choosing for that volume as a way of celebrating their work. For Sue Hufton, Brian Simpson, Susan Leiper, and Angela Swan, it was a chance to show another side of their creativity. Finally, because the script has been so important to these volumes, we will occasionally pause to look at a piece of finely executed text or points of page composition you might otherwise overlook.

A third volume of the guide will complete this series when all the volumes of *The Saint John's Bible* are finished and in house at Saint John's. At the time of this writing, the finishing touches are being put on *Historical Books*, and Donald Jackson is hard at work on *Letters and Revelation*. Each volume that arrives brings new treasures and opens new doors for contemplation and reflection on the mystery of God and the great gift of God's word. As the theme here is calling and transformation, it is our hope that this book will help you in your spiritual journey as you spend time with the words and images of *The Saint John's Bible*.

THE ART OF THE SAINT JOHN'S BIBLE

WISDOM BOOKS

I learned both what is secret and what is manifest,
for wisdom, the fashioner of all things, taught me."
(Wis 7:21-22)

W isdom Books is a very interesting part of *The Saint John's Bible* project. Most of the work of the scribes, some of whom had been with the project for six years, came to an end with the completion of the written text in this volume. *Prophets*, which is also covered by this guide, was completed first, and all of the text for *Historical Books* and for Paul's letters in the volume *Letters and Revelation* was written before the illumination in *Wisdom Books* was completed. Also, *Wisdom Books* introduces new visual themes—most significantly the figure of wisdom and the feminine aspects of the divine. In previous volumes, gold has often represented the presence of God. Silver (platinum) indicates God's female attributes throughout this volume. As mentioned in the previous volume of this guide, silver is not generally used on manuscripts because it oxidizes quickly. Impurities in the air make it blacken when exposed to the air for any length of time. For this reason, platinum leaf or powder was used almost everywhere that you see silver, unless Donald Jackson intends to seal it with something like egg white or casein lacquer.

There is great variety among the individual books, and they do not flow easily one into the other. Each book has its own feel and makes different demands on the reader and on the artists. As Donald Jackson has said, working on each volume has made him dig deeper—not just into the text but into the vocabulary of calligraphy, images, and techniques. In Wallace Stevens' poem "Of Modern Poetry" he writes of "the mind in the act of finding what will suffice." The narrator of the poem, an actor and playwright, finds that, having mastered one play, he arrives at the theater to find the stage completely changed and a new script required. He has to find what will suffice for a new audience in a new time. Tackling an illuminated, hand-written Bible for the twenty-first century is a similar task.

The nature of the wisdom books is that they collect aphorisms, verses that instruct people how to live. This literature is packed with pithy sayings. Meanwhile, Jackson was looking for a way to honor the scribes as they completed their work. He and his wife Mabel decided to commission a verse by each of the scribes. The scribes chose from a list and were given free rein over how to present their one special treatment.

The richness and variety of the art in this volume, then, reflects the richness of the team assembled for the project, and also the richness and variety in the text itself. To move from Job to Proverbs to the Song of Solomon is to see the many ways God is engaged with us—in our suffering, joy, living, loving, and dying.

Wisdom is a character in these books, a female character, and many of the books describe her in rich metaphors. In her book *Women in the Old Testament,* Irene Nowell, OSB, an Old Testament scholar and member of the Committee on Illumination and Text (CIT), writes: "She [wisdom] is the bridge between God and human beings" (139). Wisdom, then, lives among us, speaks directly to us, and if we can grab her hand she will join it to God's. In three books particularly we will see her character depicted: Proverbs, Sirach, and the Wisdom of Solomon. She is a tree, the breath of God, the firstborn and architect of creation, the Word, humankind's companion, a wife, and a bride, to be sought after and treasured when she is won. Finally, in the Wisdom of Solomon, chapter 7, it becomes clear that she is the image of God: "she is a breath of the power of God, and a pure emanation of the glory of the Almighty . . . she is a reflection of eternal light, a spotless mirror of the working of God, and an image of his goodness" (Wis 7:25-26).

Another major theme you can trace through the illuminations in this volume is creation. Again and again Donald Jackson went back to Genesis for the sources of the present illuminations. Wisdom is said to be with God at the beginning of the creation, and continues as a guide to humans as we make and remake the world in ever-expanding circles of community: families, neighborhoods, cities, countries, the globe. Again there is attentiveness to justice and compassion, as the wise enjoy the goodness of life and make that goodness available to those around them.

THE ART OF THE SAINT JOHN'S BIBLE

What do the two sides of this illumination tell us about Job?

Wisdom Books starts noisily. In this illumination we see not Job himself but rather a portrayal of his world, which is quite clearly in chaos. On the left side of the illumination we see Job's riches: his cattle, donkeys, camels, servants. There are also the signs of fertility in the birds and fish at the bottom of the panel, and the arches of buildings at the top. But notice, the animals and servants are facing away, already walking off-stage, led into captivity by Job's enemies. By the center of the illumination things are starting to come down. Here are fire and the fractures we associate with chaos. Looking back to the first panel in the Genesis illumination for creation, you will see the same harsh quality to the swaths of color. By the right-hand side of the panel all is lost, and there remains the black and purple of richness undone by tragedy. Only slender bars of gold remain to tell Job that God is still present.

This illumination can also be read from top left down to bottom right, to trace Job's spiritual journey. In *Wisdom Books* we see a new representation of the presence of divinity. In other volumes divinity has been represented by gold and also, in *Prophets*, by rainbows. Wisdom is another way the divine is present, and it is marked by silver. In the top left you will see chunks of silver along with gold, a sign of Job's closeness to God, his possession of wisdom and God's favor. Through the center of the illumination the bars turn to black, there

Job Frontispiece

JOB 1–2
There was once a man in the land of Uz whose name was Job. (1:1)

JOB FRONTISPIECE

is less gold, and God seems very far from Job. Finally, though, at the bottom right he receives a full measure of wisdom and reconnection to God's presence. The gold and silver bars return, along with gold stamps. Job's life is once again permeated with an awareness of God's presence.

Another visual motif seen for the first time in *Wisdom Books* is introduced at the top right of the illumination. It is a stamp based on an astronomical chart from an ancient Islamic work. The astronomical chart shows how we try to penetrate the mysteries of the world with our mind. From ancient times, humans have always used reason—and art—to describe the world. Those forces come together in charts like this. Like Job and his friends, we seek answers and try to contain what we know in visual representations. Our knowledge is always limited, our ways of grasping the central concepts of creation are always creative themselves—sense-making, ordering, but also merely representative of the whole truth that remains beyond our grasp, the work and being of God.

The quotation on the opposite page is from one of Job's early responses to his suffering: "Shall we receive the good at the hand of God and not receive the bad?" Job loses everything in these opening passages, but he maintains his confidence in God. He speaks with wisdom here.

Below the verse is a piece of another new stamp made for *Wisdom Books*. The pattern is based on a piece of cloth from India embroidered and appliquéd with mirrors. This stamp will be used to make the tree of wisdom in later illuminations. Mirrors are at the heart of another important illumination, *Wisdom Woman*. This vision of wisdom is geometrical, ordered and ordering, complex and delicate. Wisdom reflects truth to us, and is beautiful and complex. As we shall see, wisdom is a reflection of the feminine qualities of God.

Finally, note should be taken of the *incipit,* the opening passage. Donald Jackson wrote this passage, and he says it is his best piece of writing in the completed five volumes. Other scribes have commented on the accomplishment of this beautifully written passage as well. Although we might

אִיוֹב

JOB

THERE WAS ONCE A MAN
IN THE LAND OF UZ
WHOSE NAME WAS JOB.
THAT MAN WAS BLAMELESS
AND UPRIGHT, ONE WHO
FEARED GOD AND TURNED
AWAY FROM EVIL. THERE WERE
BORN TO HIM SEVEN SONS AND
THREE DAUGHTERS. HE HAD
SEVEN THOUSAND SHEEP,
THREE THOUSAND CAMELS,
FIVE HUNDRED YOKE OF OXEN,
FIVE HUNDRED DONKEYS, AND
VERY MANY SERVANTS; SO
THAT THIS MAN WAS THE
GREATEST OF ALL THE PEOPLE
OF THE EAST. HIS SONS USED TO
GO AND HOLD FEASTS IN ONE
ANOTHER'S HOUSES IN TURN;
AND THEY WOULD SEND AND
INVITE THEIR THREE SISTERS TO
EAT AND DRINK WITH THEM.
AND WHEN THE FEAST DAYS
HAD RUN THEIR COURSE, JOB
WOULD SEND AND SANCTIFY
THEM, AND HE WOULD RISE
EARLY IN THE MORNING AND
OFFER BURNT OFFERINGS
ACCORDING TO THE NUMBER
OF THEM ALL; FOR JOB SAID, "IT
MAY BE THAT MY CHILDREN
HAVE SINNED, AND CURSED
GOD IN THEIR HEARTS." THIS IS
WHAT JOB ALWAYS DID.

⁶ One day the heavenly beings came to present
themselves before the LORD, and Satan also came
among them. The LORD said to Satan, "Where
have you come from?" Satan answered the LORD,
"From going to & fro on the earth, and from walking
up and down on it." ⁸ The LORD said to Satan,
"Have you considered my servant Job? There is no
one like him on the earth, a blameless & upright
man who fears God and turns away from evil."

⁹ Then Satan answered the LORD, "Does Job fear God
for nothing? ¹⁰ Have you not put a fence around him
and his house and all that he has, on every side? You
have blessed the work of his hands, and his posses-
sions have increased in the land." ¹¹ But stretch out
your hand now, and touch all that he has, and he
will curse you to your face." ¹² The LORD said to Satan,
"Very well, all that he has is in your power; only do
not stretch out your hand against him!" So Satan
went out from the presence of the LORD. ¹³ One day
when his sons & daughters were eating and drinking wine in the eldest brother's house, ¹⁴ a messenger
came to Job and said, "The oxen were plowing and
the donkeys were feeding beside them, ¹⁵ and the
Sabeans fell on them & carried them off, and killed
the servants with the edge of the sword; I alone have
escaped to tell you." ¹⁶ While he was still speaking,
another came and said, "The fire of God fell from
heaven and burned up the sheep and the servants,
and consumed them; I alone have escaped to tell
you." ¹⁷ While he was still speaking, another came
and said, "The Chaldeans formed three columns,
made a raid on the camels and carried them off,
and killed the servants with the edge of the sword;
I alone have escaped to tell you." ¹⁸ While he was still
speaking, another came and said; Your sons and
daughters were eating and drinking wine in their
eldest brother's house, ¹⁹ and suddenly a great wind
came across the desert, struck the four corners of
the house, and it fell on the young people, and they
²⁰ are dead; I alone have escaped to tell you." Then
Job arose, tore his robe, shaved his head, and fell on
the ground and worshiped. ²¹ He said, "Naked I came
from my mother's womb, and naked shall I return
there; the LORD gave, and the LORD has taken away;
²² blessed be the name of the LORD." In all this Job
did not sin or charge God with wrongdoing.

2

One day the heavenly beings came to present themselves before the LORD, and Satan also came among
them to present himself before the LORD. ² The LORD
said to Satan, "Where have you come from?" Satan
answered the LORD, "From going to and fro on the
earth, and from walking up and down on it." ³ The
LORD said to Satan, "Have you considered my servant Job? There is no one like him on the earth, a
blameless & upright man who fears God and turns
away from evil. He still persists in his integrity, although you incited me against him to destroy him
for no reason." ⁴ Then Satan answered the LORD, "Skin
for skin! All that people have they will give to save
their lives. ⁵ But stretch out your hand now, and touch

SHALL WE RECEIVE THE GOOD AT THE HAND OF GOD, AND NOT RECEIVE THE BAD?

1.6 *Heb* sons of God
b c d e f g h j k l m n
Or the Adversary; *Heb* ha-
satan
⁴ *Or* All that the man has
he will give for his life

not recognize it, this form of writing is much different from the calligraphy of the body text. The calligrapher is not using a standard "script" (comparable to what we think of as a font in the printed world) to tell him or her how to shape and space the letters. The process is more open, more intuitive. Although this kind of writing is plotted out on the computer beforehand, it is closer to a text treatment. You can say it is less craft and more art, though there is always a balance of the two in calligraphy. For a comparison, look at the *incipits* for the four gospels. Matthew, Mark, and John open with long written passages. It is hard to find fault with these pieces of writing, and the subtle differences between pieces of text are part of the art. The capitals are written in an improvisatory spirit. Note the variety of *A*'s, *H*'s, *Z*'s and *E*'s, and how some letters are flowed into each other to maintain spacing and rhythm. Many things contribute to making a good piece of calligraphy—the quality of the particular sheet of vellum, the cooperation of the ink and quill, the length and shape of the passage, and the focus and feeling of the artist on a particular day.

❧ *Looking back on the illumination, what do you think about its representation of the presence of divinity in a time of loss?*

THE ART OF THE SAINT JOHN'S BIBLE

On the margins of the text for Job 15 is the first of the five scribal text treatments. This one is by Angela Swan and is actually the verse Wisdom of Solomon 6:12. The five scribes chose their text treatments from a list of verses that emphasized the female character of Wisdom as personified in the books. They do not always appear alongside the text to which they refer, which is unusual for the project. They are spaced as evenly as possible throughout the volume to maintain the feminine emphasis in the margins of the plain text pages.

This first treatment is fairly simple and straightforward. A master calligrapher, Angela Swan lets the words speak for themselves. Brian Simpson also focused on the lettering, and his treatment of Sirach 1:16 has a simple and elegant bold-ness. Sally Mae Joseph, who has done a lot of ornamental work on the project and other text treatments, adorned her chosen text, Sirach 24:19 (found at Sir 13), with a jaunty flower. There is a similarity between this piece and her later text treatment at the opening of the book of Ezekiel. More unusual is the treatment by Susie Leiper of Wisdom 7:26 (found at Sir 35). Her work is heavily influenced by the time she spent in Hong Kong and China, reflecting ideas of light and dark and balance. Here the yin-yang symbol adorns her treatment, which is written on a field of silver and black. Finally, the treatment by Sue Hufton, Sirach 24:12, 13, 15-17 (found at Sir 44), focuses primarily on the space of the page. The words, painted with a fine brush and separated by deftly applied flecks of powdered gold ink, are like wafting incense or vines of abundant fruit. They carry us to the incense of the temple interior in Isaiah's vision, and the abundance of Ezekiel's Vision of the New Temple.

Commissioned Text Treatments

WISDOM
IS
RADIANT
AND
UNFADING
AND SHE
IS EASILY
DISCERNED
BY THOSE
WHO
LOVE HER
AND IS
FOUND
BY THOSE
WHO
SEEK HER

WISDOM 6:12

JOB 38–42
Shall a faultfinder contend
with the Almighty? (40:2)

After reading these chapters, can you summarize God's
answer to Job in a sentence or two? Is it what you were
expecting?

At the end of Job is a complex, three-part illumination by Thomas Ingmire. Ingmire struggled with this assignment, which is indeed difficult. God's answer to Job is hard to take. Ingmire joined the project as an artist and calligrapher, primarily concerned with the visual potential of words. Still, these are not isolated words, and one demand of the assignment is to engage with the text in its context. This famous story of Job aims to give God's answer to questions about suffering. We expect the answer to tell us something about what kind of god this YHWH is. And Ingmire's previous assignments for *The Saint John's Bible* have engaged him directly with the question of who God is. The *Ten Commandments* (Gen 20), *I AM Sayings* (John 6–15), and *Messianic Predictions* (Isa 9), directly engage the announcement of God's names and God's relationship with humanity. What to do, then, with God's answer to Job?

Another challenge was that this passage covers more or less the same ground as the frontispiece for Job. Donald Jackson took the material and decided to generalize and set the tone/mood. Thomas Ingmire has focused on the text and quotations, drawing more attention to the questions raised by Job and by the text, and to God's answer.

God answers Job's pleas for an explanation not with consolation but with questions—questions and demands that sound like accusations to our ear. "Respond," "Tell me," "Where were you when I laid the foundation of the earth?" The voice from the whirlwind is booming and relentless, speaking for four chapters. Ingmire focused his illumination on the words coming out of the whirlwind, shouting capital letters pouring from everywhere, overlapping, insistent, without pause. They are rhetorical: "Can you draw out Leviathan with a fishhook?" But God wants a response: "I will question you, and you shall declare to me." In what seems like an unsympathetic reply, God evokes his own

¹⁶"Have you entered into the springs of the sea,
or walked in the recesses of the deep?
¹⁷Have the gates of death been revealed to you,
or have you seen the gates of deep darkness?
¹⁸Have you comprehended the expanse
of the earth?
Declare, if you know all this.

¹⁹"Where is the way to the dwelling of light,
and where is the place of darkness,
²⁰that you may take it to its territory
and that you may discern the
paths to its home?
²¹Surely you know, for you were born then,
and the number of your days is great!

²²"Have you entered the storehouses
of the snow,
or have you seen the storehouses of the hail,
²³which I have reserved for the time of trouble,
for the day of battle and war?
²⁴What is the way to the place where
the light is distributed,
or where the east wind is scattered
upon the earth?

²⁵"Who has cut a channel for the torrents of rain,
and a way for the thunderbolt,
²⁶to bring rain on a land where no one lives,
on the desert, which is empty of human life,
²⁷to satisfy the waste and desolate land,
and to make the ground put forth grass?

²⁸"Has the rain a father,
or who has begotten the drops of dew?
²⁹From whose womb did the ice come forth,
and who has given birth to the
hoarfrost of heaven?
³⁰The waters become hard like stone,
and the face of the deep is frozen.

Meaning of Heb uncertain

³¹"Can you bind the chains of the Pleiades,
or loose the cords of Orion?
³²Can you lead forth the Mazzaroth
in their season,
or can you guide the Bear with its children?
³³Do you know the ordinances of the heavens?
Can you establish their rule on the earth?

³⁴"Can you lift up your voice to the clouds,
so that a flood of waters may cover you?
³⁵Can you send forth lightnings
so that they may go
and say to you, 'Here we are'?
³⁶Who has put wisdom in the inward parts,
or given understanding to the mind?
³⁷Who has the wisdom to number the clouds?
Or who can tilt the waterskins
of the heavens,
³⁸when the dust runs into a mass
and the clods cling together?

³⁹"Can you hunt the prey for the lion,
or satisfy the appetite of the young lions,
⁴⁰when they crouch in their dens,
or lie in wait in their covert?
⁴¹Who provides for the raven its prey,
when its young ones cry to God,
and wander about for lack of food?

OUT OF THE WHIRLWIND—WHERE WERE YOU

OUT OF THE WHIRLWIND—
NOW MY EYE SEES YOU

power and majesty in his answer to Job. God, the creator of the universe and all that is in it, has reasons the human mind cannot fathom or plumb, and he tells Job so.

Finally, the roar is interrupted by the simple and faint lines uttered by Job: "I had heard of you by the hearing of the ear, but now my eye sees you" (Job 42:5). We too have seen God in the whirlwind, in Ingmire's calligraphic treatment of God's words. But how do we feel about this God? Is not this the fearful Old Testament God booming judgment from the heavens? How can God be angry with his faithful servant who has lost everything, been badgered by his friends, and simply given in to despair?

This is not the end of the story, as the final piece in Job by Ingmire illustrates. However, he retains the tension in this final piece. The illumination is structured like *Messianic Predictions* in *Prophets*, with strings of words like trumpet blasts. However, unlike the words announcing the names of the Messiah, these sentences from the beginning of the book of Job announce destruction. "The fire of God fell from heaven and killed the servants." "A great wind came across the desert, struck the four corners of the house, and it fell on the young people and they are dead." Alongside a column of text that recounts Job's satisfaction with God's answer, we are reminded of all he has lost. And the blame is placed squarely on "the fire of God." This time, however, the words of destruction are laid on a quite different foun-

THE ART OF THE SAINT JOHN'S BIBLE

dation. Even in the midst of the chronicle of devastation, Job's answer begins: "I know that you can do all things, and that no purpose of yours can be thwarted."

And the foundation of this illumination, a colorful wall of words, is the comfort we have waited for. Ingmire has rested the book of Job on Revelation 21:4, a scriptural cross-reference suggested by the CIT. It is messianic and eschatological, referring to that place beyond human suffering that we cannot grasp but that we know awaits us. "He will wipe every tear from their eyes. / Death will be no more; / mourning and crying and pain will be no more, / for the first things have passed away." The answer, he seems to be saying, is not even here in this particular book, but only beyond this text will the answers be revealed.

Scholars have often minimized the passage that restores all Job's goods and riches to him. What matters here is the wisdom of accepting that God's ways are higher than humanity's ways. The words of the final illumination

OUT OF THE WHIRLWIND—HE WILL WIPE EVERY TEAR

seem to play on the idea of Job's "replacement" riches, that he is given all that he had before and more. At this time in salvation history there was no concept of heaven, of an afterlife where the ones who died would get their reward. Job's long life and his ability to see four generations of his family born into prosperity offer a parallel to Christian images of eternal life.

❦ *In what ways has God "spoken" to you in your life? What phrases might you put in place of the words in these illuminations as a conversation with God?*

The Fear of the Lord Is the Beginning of Knowledge

PROVERBS 1:7-8

Do you know any proverbs? If so, where do they come from? Where did you learn them?

Thomas Ingmire also created the illumination that opens the book of Proverbs. It directly references his illumination of Isaiah 66:12-13 in *Prophets*. That illumination compares Jerusalem to a nursing mother and promises that the day will come when the people will be comforted and nurtured again at home. The next verse elaborates on this image, describing God's relationship with Israel as maternal: "As a mother comforts her child, so I will comfort you" (Isa 66:13). Feminine images of God, like this one in Isaiah, are central in *Wisdom Books*.

We are introduced to Wisdom as a female character in Proverbs. She appears here first as a street prophet: "Wisdom cries out in the street; in the squares she raises her voice" (1:20). The book of Proverbs is a series of instructions from a couple to their son. We begin: "The fear of the LORD is the beginning of knowledge; fools despise wisdom and instruction. Hear, my child, your father's instruction, and do not reject your mother's teaching." They will tell him stories about this woman Wisdom, and encourage him to court and eventually marry her, while warning again and again about the dangers of infidelity and that bad woman, Folly.

On the original vellum pages Ingmire produced an interesting effect that only comes through faintly in the reproduction. There is considerable "show-through" from the back page, which of course is his final illumination for the book of Job. On the reproductions you can make out some of the columns and arcs from the back of the page, but much of the show-through has been lost in the reproduction process. The modern eye often finds show-through untidy and distracting—a mistake—whereas earlier readers of handmade books accepted these "shadows" as a foretaste of what was to come. The rhythm and continuity of our experience of the book is enhanced by these images caused by the materials themselves.

On the actual page (and in the Heritage Edition, where show-through has been selectively restored) the show-through is dramatic, and you can even make out words announcing the destruction of Job's family and belongings, although of course they appear in reverse. It is as though Ingmire does not want us to forget that there is a limit to wisdom and knowledge. Remember what God said to Job: No matter how much knowledge you have, God's ways are higher. Now we read: "The fear of the LORD is the *beginning* of knowledge."

To fully understand what Ingmire is commenting on, read further in Proverbs. Proverbs 1:24-33, in fact, sounds like Job's friends, who indeed do represent the worldview of their time. The parents advise that the ones who love Wisdom, like Job, "will be secure and will live at ease, without dread of disaster" (Prov 1:33). But the ones who ignore Wisdom will be struck down. In fact, in the book of Job his friends used exactly this logic to argue that Job must have done something wrong to deserve his suffering. They are pious people who live by the worldview represented in Proverbs. The righteous are rewarded and the wicked are punished. Look at what Wisdom says in Proverbs 1:26-27: "I will mock when panic strikes you [the wicked], when panic strikes you like a storm, and your calamity comes like a whirlwind." Wait a minute! Didn't God indeed scold Job from a whirlwind? Ingmire's heavy show-through on the page tells us to remember Job. However, how are we to read these seemingly contradictory passages? We should hold onto the complexity, and realize that much of the truth in the Bible is in the tension between God's ways and human experience. The truth is contained within the interplay of the two statements.

PROVERBS 1:7-8

Seven Pillars of Wisdom

PROVERBS 8:22–9:6
*In the scripture passage and
the illumination, how is
Wisdom's creativity
portrayed?*

Wisdom has built her house, she has hewn her seven pillars. (9:1)

This passage gives more detail about who Wisdom is and how she works. The NRSV compares Proverbs 8:22-31 with John 1:1-3. "In the beginning," in other words, there was also Wisdom. Many read this as an allusion to Wisdom as the preexistent Word of God, which Christians see as Christ. Wisdom plays a part in creation, and "when [God] marked out the foundations of the earth, then I was beside him, like a master worker; and I was daily his delight, rejoicing before him always, rejoicing in his inhabited world and delighting in the human race" (Prov 8:29-31). Chapter 9 continues by telling of the feast Wisdom has prepared for those who wish to follow her ways. Creation and banquet are a potent combination, and they come together in the magnificent illumination by Donald Jackson.

Seven is a symbolic number in the Old Testament, signifying completion or fullness. There is a perfection and fullness to the created order of Wisdom's world. On each of the pillars is an orb, a pearl, a precious thing of beauty created by mysterious processes. It also makes us think of "pearls of wisdom," the compact truths found throughout Proverbs. Finally, the orbs are reminiscent of that heavenly body associated with feminine forces, the moon.

The tree of wisdom takes center stage, based on the fabric sample adorned with mirrors. Growing from another pillar is a complex of buildings, themselves built on columns and arches and with a series of arched roofs. According to Donald Jackson, the buildings "just grew" from one another as he worked. Among the buildings on the upper left hand of the page is tucked a monochromatic green drawing of the dome of the church at Saint Benedict's Monastery. Just four miles down the road from Saint John's Monastery, Saint Benedict's was founded as a sister monastery in 1857 and is also home to the College of Saint Benedict. The distinguished scholar and artist Johanna Becker, OSB, is a member of Saint Benedict's monastic community and a member of the CIT.

The cosmos stretches overhead, acknowledging Wisdom's part in creation. Images of the cosmos and space ap-

SEVEN PILLARS OF WISDOM

pear throughout *The Saint John's Bible,* from *Creation* in Genesis to the final illumination of *Gospels and Acts, To the Ends of the Earth.* Again in the sky a piece of the wisdom tree, here looking more like one of the heavenly bodies, reveals Wisdom's presence. Wisdom is with us and beyond us, accessible to humans in the world around us but also greater than our minds can grasp. The masculine and the feminine are both here, but the emphasis is on the traditionally female moon and stars, creativity.

A table is set with wine and bread on the right-hand page of the illumination. This image comes out of the text, but it makes yet another connection between Wisdom and Christ. The invitation to "Come, eat of my bread and drink of the wine I have mixed" resonates with the invitation of the eucharistic prayer.

One verse on the page stands out here because it is written in red instead of black. You will notice the cross in the margin that tells us this verse is used in the Rule of Benedict. This verse and Proverbs 15:3 both appear multiple times in the Rule of Benedict, and so get slightly heavier treatment here.

Hymn to a Virtuous Woman

PROVERBS 31:1-31
Charm is deceitful, and beauty is vain, but a woman who fears the LORD is to be praised. (31:30)

HYMN TO A VIRTUOUS WOMAN

Which of these virtues are still relevant, and which seem outdated?

The book of Proverbs ends with a hymn to the value of a good wife. This wife may be Wisdom herself, who has been sought throughout the book. The hymn closes out a book of instruction to a young man, and logically ends with advice on what kind of woman to marry. This passage also marks a shift in speaker—it is the mother, not the father, who gives the son this advice.

This illumination by Hazel Dolby is in the form of a sampler or tapestry, such as may be found decorating a home. Many of the aphorisms in Proverbs have been rendered decoratively as concrete words to live by. Embroidery is traditionally a woman's art, and this illumination draws attention to the place of women in ethical instruction. The images themselves have a domestic quality, including water jugs, gardens, and quilt patterns. The treatment draws attention to God's domesticity, helping us see God as a nurturer who looks after the well-being of the home. Order and creation, as well as creativity and care, are among the ways we see God's presence reflected in our daily lives. The illumination also extends to the margins, framing the whole page with images of flowers, a vase, and a bee working a honeycomb. Another delicate detail is the tassels on the bottom. These are like the tassels on the hem of a Jewish prayer shawl that are meant to be a specific reminder to the wearer to pray and remember God's blessings.

❦ *What qualities do you look for in friends? If you wrote a hymn praising the virtues of someone you know, what qualities would you sing?*

What "messengers" between the human world and God do you see here? What do you think their significance is?

Ecclesiastes
Frontispiece

Ecclesiastes seems in some ways a return to Job. Here again the big questions are taken up: what gives life meaning? What hope can there be when the wise and the foolish suffer the same fate in the end? Here the author, a philosopher giving his name as Qoheleth (in Latin "Ecclesiastes"), takes on the *persona* of Solomon. He gives voice to the feelings we had when turning from Job to the opening of Proverbs: "I applied my mind to know wisdom and to know madness and folly. I perceived that this is also but a chasing after wind. For in much wisdom is much vexation, and those who increase knowledge increase sorrow" (1:17-18). It is death that is troubling this author. There is an old saying that only two things are certain: death and taxes. Never mind the taxes, says the author of Ecclesiastes, how can we go on living when we know that what lies before us is death?

ECCLESIASTES I
Vanity of vanities! All is vanity. (1:2b)

The author is not the first to ask this question, and will not be the last. Scholars see direct parallels between the structure and message of Ecclesiastes and the earliest known piece of writing, Gilgamesh. The opening poetry resonates in Hamlet's famous soliloquy, "To be or not to be, that is the question." Dostoevsky asks the question repeatedly through his characters and their moral struggles. Woody Allen takes it up in *Hannah and Her Sisters,* where a character who gets a reprieve from a terminal diagnosis loses all sense of meaning and purpose, realizing the reprieve can only be temporary. He regains his sense of life's meaning in a dark theater while watching the Marx brothers—why not enjoy life while we're here; after all, there is so much to enjoy.

In fact, this is the very conclusion drawn by the fictitious speaker, Solomon, in 2:24-26. "There is nothing better for mortals than to eat and drink, and find enjoyment in their toil." This joy, too, the wise man says, is the gift of God. In the end, the philosopher advises: "The end of the matter: all has been heard. Fear God, and keep his commandments; for that is the whole duty of everyone" (12:13). This is a

confounding little book, which can be read as very pessimistic but also as very hopeful. The wise person lives following God, and finds peace, freedom, and joy in the very understanding that everything is in God's hands. For the modern existentialist reader, however, the book confirms: Why bother? Things are in God's hands, not mine.

Ecclesiastes' frontispiece sees the return of many elements from Genesis. This is appropriate because Ecclesiastes, like so much in the wisdom books, focuses attention on life and death and the place of God in human life.

Most prominent is the raven flying up from the center of the illumination. The raven traversed the illumination *Creation*. Donald Jackson has said that birds are messengers, and this one, also a common symbol of death, seems to carry the breath of life back to God. Still, it is pierced and surrounded by gold and silver bars, designations of divinity in male and female form.

Other messengers are present as well, seraph wings that will play a prominent role in *Prophets*. The sometimes frightening guardians of God as king are present. The bars of rainbow color are another sign of God's presence, God's ongoing covenant, asserting itself against the otherwise chaotic image of the cosmos. Human intelligence also asserts itself here in the image of the ancient Islamic astronomical chart. Here is another place where the mind attempts to grasp things that really cannot be fully comprehended. Trusting in the divine and remembering that in the midst of chaos the divine is present may be the only way to soothe the person engaged with these questions.

Finally, the shattered butterfly wings by Chris Tomlin take us back to *Jacob's Ladder* (Gen 28:10-22) and *Jacob's Dream* (Gen 32:24-32). Butterflies are also creatures who bridge both worlds, the human and the divine. Beautiful and mysterious, they remind us of God's skill in creation. In fragments here, they speak to us of chaos as well as metamorphosis—life to death and death to life.

The elements of creation are all here: the green of the earth, the blue of water, the sky with its dusting of stars and images of comets. But the elements are disrupted, chaotic, circling or spinning off the page. Donald Jackson was asked to create a sense of vortex sucking inwards as well as its opposite, entropic forces spinning outwards into the universe. God is present and in communication between the heavens and the earth. All of this is overshadowed by the speaker's gloom, however, as he proclaims across the top of the page, "and the breath returns to God who gave it" (Eccl 12:7).

Garden of Desire

What role does desire play in our lives? In our prayers?

SONG OF SOLOMON
4:12–5:8
*A garden locked is my sister,
my bride, a garden locked, a
fountain sealed. (4:12)*

I give you the end of a golden string,
Only wind it into a ball;
It will lead you in at Heaven's gate,
Built in Jerusalem's wall.

William Blake, "Jerusalem"

This quotation from early-nineteenth-century British poet and mystic William Blake could be applied to the illumination of the vision of the temple in Ezekiel, but it also seems apt here. Throughout the Song of Solomon, the literal love poem and the allegory of the love between God and Israel play out in rich and evocative images that also have layers of meaning. Wisdom is a personified quality we seek and hope to catch, and that ultimately leads us to communion with God. In the illumination here of a walled garden we find a type of labyrinth. Later we will see a labyrinth in the temple vision of Ezekiel. At the heart of our exploration of Wisdom in this literature and these illuminations is the search for a closeness with God we can attain here on earth. As the groom is lured toward the garden by the scent of its fruit trees and spices, so are we drawn by Wisdom, as if winding up a ball of golden string, until we reach heaven's gate. In the same way an herb garden behind a kitchen draws us in with its scents, fresh greenery, and the order of its geometric plantings, to the delights of those waiting to greet us and nourish us on the other side of the door.

The scattered elements of gold and deep red draw attention to our disconnection from God. Like pieces of a jigsaw puzzle, they desire to be reunited within the formal garden and thus become whole. If they could be assembled, they would make up a parterre, a formal garden design using flower beds, hedges, stone walls, and other elements. They represent our longing for oneness with the divine.

The Song of Solomon, called in other translations Song of Songs, reminds us again of the variety found in the wisdom books. It is quite clearly a collection of love songs sung by a man and a woman and is full of playful eroticism. Aside

THE ART OF THE SAINT JOHN'S BIBLE

from the quality of the lyric poetry, what recommended it for inclusion in the sacred canon? There are no really good answers to this question. However, the Song of Solomon certainly fits with what we have learned from the wisdom books so far. It is a balance to the darker questions of suffering, loss, and death. You can imagine the young student invoked in Proverbs 1 asking: "What about love?" And if Wisdom advises that enjoyment of life is a gift from God, why not a brief book celebrating romantic love, one of life's greatest pleasures?

The Song was probably sung at banquets on religious feasts, and today passages from it are read at weddings. In later times the book came to be read as an allegory for the relationship between Israel and God or the church and God. However, there is no getting away from the fact that these poems were written not as allegory but as love songs. Like Proverbs and the other wisdom books, this one was probably

GARDEN OF DESIRE

not written by Solomon. As the king's court would have been responsible for assembling anthologies of wisdom, they also assembled collections of poetry. The phrase "song of songs" in Hebrew is a superlative—this is the best of all possible songs. Solomon's name gives the book authority.

The opportunity to find a visual language for this poetry was picked up enthusiastically by Donald Jackson. There is definitely the highest ratio of illumination to text in this book! Two back-to-back spreads and a text treatment adorn the eight chapters of poetry.

The garden imagery, warm colors, and butterfly, all done by Donald Jackson, separate this book from Ecclesiastes starting right at the book title. Chris Tomlin was on another assignment, so Donald Jackson painted this butterfly. Mosaic pieces of the parterre dance on this page. Turning the page, we enter more fully into the garden where the lovers look for each other. The image is also used to describe the beloved: "A garden locked is my sister, my bride, a garden locked, a fountain sealed" (4:12).

In this illumination are order and disorder, beauty and pattern and incompletion. The red circle with walls around it is taken from a design of a Middle Eastern garden. Jackson has deliberately left it unfinished, only two gates mapped out, asymmetrical. The courtship of these lovers balances the passion that sends her out into the street at night to find him and the propriety that observes the conventions of marriage and warns again and again, "do not stir up or awaken love until it is ready!" (2:7; 3:1-5). Until their union is complete, there is something off-balance about the scene. The margin makes use of stamps again in warm colors, and fills in the garden with trees and flowers. The place is warm and inviting, a sanctuary of earthly delights. Finally, another color motif in this book is found in the verse numbers. Three colors are used to signify the alternation between the speakers: the man, the woman, and another speaker marked "unidentified," often interpreted as the chorus of daughters of Jerusalem. The color key is in the marginal notes of the pages where the speakers' verses appear.

How does your reading of the Song of Solomon affect your understanding or appreciation of the Bible as a whole?

The two-page spread titled *I Am My Beloved's* maintains the idea of a border or boundary from the last illumination, this time in lilac, yellow, and gold. The border here was not made with stamps but with pieces of lace dipped in paint and pow-

I AM MY BELOVED'S

dered gold ink, a less precise technique to say the least. Warm colors are used for the rather abstract lilies and the block of color behind the text. The gold of divine presence, which has previously appeared in blocks or bars, here appears as petals or seeds. In making the lilies, Donald Jackson tipped his board and let the paint dribble or run down the page to make the stems, only marking off areas of text before he guided it. It was a frightening moment for someone working with these materials, the one-time-only chance to

SET ME AS A SEAL UPON
YOUR HEART

get it right with so much of the work on the page already completed. If one can't take risks in the Song of Solomon, however, where can one? The technique gives in to the abandon and single-mindedness, the "fierceness" of love with which the two lovers seek out each other. As with so much of this volume of *The Saint John's Bible*, the focus here is on the words, our attention drawn to the columns of poetry and not distracted by elaborately detailed images. The little blue and yellow butterflies were painted by Sarah Harris. Where the team members could be incorporated they were, and this volume is a testament to the collaboration, some of which was coming to an end with this volume.

On the back of the page is a text treatment. The passionate verses read: "Set me as a seal upon your heart, as a seal upon your arm; for love is strong as death, passion fierce as the grave. Its flashes are flashes of fire, a raging flame. Many waters cannot quench love, neither can floods drown it. If one offered for love all the wealth of one's house, it would be utterly scorned" (Song 8:6-7). The passage is written not with a quill but with a reed pen. The split reed is light and writes like a quill pen dipped in paint except that its woody edge creates softer shapes. Donald Jackson says you have to keep it moving and get into a rhythm with it. What he wanted was an earthly, primitive feel, emphasized by the variations of color seen here. It exhibits yet another possibility in the techniques of the ancient art of writing.

The Song of Solomon has a long history in monastic traditions. Bernard of Clairvaux, a Benedictine of the twelfth century, wrote a series of beautiful sermons on the book. Bernard was a great reformer and founder of the Cistercian movement, known for its austerity and strict adherence to the Rule of Benedict. It says a lot about Benedictines that the founder of this community so embraced the passionate Song of Solomon. The purpose of monastic life, after all, is to seek out God as the beloved and to live in God's embrace.

THE ART OF THE SAINT JOHN'S BIBLE

Can you think of contemporary films or books that might be reflections of this story of those who pursue folly instead of wisdom?

Let Us Lie in Wait

WISDOM OF SOLOMON
1:16–2:24
Let us lie in wait for the righteous man, because he is inconvenient to us. (2:12)

The starkness and violence of this illumination lets us know something is up. There is no garden here, no tapestry, no meal. Worse yet, the text appears to be written backwards on the page. Most likely you did not identify this as the work of Thomas Ingmire, although we've seen several of his pieces in this very volume. Whereas pleasing, bright colors and meticulous geometrical patterns have marked his previous contributions, this one is done just in black and gold. It appears scratched and smudged in places. There is the hint of vertical panels, as in the *Ten Commandments* and the *I AM Sayings*, but they do not come out even or help us make sense of what is going on.

At the same time, this passage in Wisdom of Solomon speaks to the exact issue raised in Ecclesiastes. Of course, it does so "in reverse," not through the eyes of the wise man but through the wrong reasoning of the ungodly. It takes the wisdom of Ecclesiastes, that we should enjoy life as a

LET US LIE IN WAIT

gift from God, and subverts it. In Wisdom 1:16–2:24 we are shown the thinking of the ungodly, those who "reasoned unsoundly" and decided that since life on earth was all there is, they should live for pleasure. Further, their unsound reasoning gives them license to "oppress the righteous poor man" and the widow, allowing "might [to] be our law of right" (2:10-11). Ultimately this passage begins to resonate with the story of Christ's Passion. The ungodly behave like those in the gospels who follow Jesus around in order to trip him up and eventually kill him. So we see in Ingmire's illumination the "backward" text: "Let us lie in wait for the righteous man" (2:12). The ungodly live in a two-tone world, mostly black, and do not see God. They bring violence and chaos into the world. They are without wisdom.

The verse in the frame tells us the error of the ungodly: "They did not know the secret purposes of God . . . for God created us for incorruption, and made us in the image of his own eternity" (vv. 22a, 23). The crucifixion, paradoxically, carries out God's "secret purposes," God's ultimate plan. Remember the words of Job? "I know that you can do all things, and that no purpose of yours can be thwarted" (Job 42:2). As Paul wrote, "We know that all things work together for good for those who love God, who are called according to his purpose" (Rom 8:28). It is only with this faith that we live in the knowledge of true wisdom and avoid the despair of both Job and the author of Ecclesiastes.

Scholars now believe the Wisdom of Solomon influenced the formation of the New Testament. In addition to this prefigurement of the passion narrative, they also look at the description of Wisdom in chapters 6, 7, and 10, particularly as the agent for God's creation. As Proverbs 8 spoke of Wisdom's presence and role in creation, so this book reinforces the idea of a preexistent Christ, important to the theology of the Trinity. Even more, with the focus on the feminine pronoun and female attributes it expands our conception of Christ from the historical Jesus to include a more complex set of images to contemplate God as creator, savior, and God with us.

What are the attributes of Wisdom you see reflected in this mirror? Do they match the discussions so far of Wisdom personified as a woman?

This illumination accompanies the prayer of Solomon, the wise king and son of David, the builder of the temple, who calls on God to send Wisdom to help him. The passage again stresses the eternal nature of Wisdom, who was there at the beginning when the heavens and earth were made. Wisdom is seen as a guide who will labor by Solomon's side.

The motif of the mirror comes to full fruition in this illumination, with the face of Wisdom reflected in a mirror. As mentioned earlier, it is in this book that Wisdom is elevated to full divinity. We read in chapter 7: "For she is a breath of the power of God, and a pure emanation of the glory of the Almighty . . . she is a reflection of eternal light, a spotless mirror of the working of God, an image of his goodness" (7:25-26). We can never see God directly in this life, but in Wisdom we see God's reflection in the mirror— and it is a female face we see.

A photograph of a Palestinian woman inspired this image. The only other time actual human faces appear in *The Saint John's Bible* is in Genesis, with Adam and Eve. In fact, it is worth going back to that image with its mirrored background (hard to make out in the reproduction), which was accompanied by a quotation from the letter to the Romans: "And all of us with unveiled faces seeing the glory of the Lord as though reflected in a mirror, are being transformed into the same image from one degree of glory to another" (Rom 8:19). The mirror connects both images as well as the idea of humanity created in God's image and reflecting God's glory.

The image of the woman's face was silk-screened onto the vellum multiple times. Silk-screening was a terrifying process for Donald Jackson and the team because of its unforgiving nature. You get one pull over the screen and hope for the best. This composition was made more difficult because it spans two separate sheets of vellum. The pages fit together in such a way that half of the image is on one sheet while the other half is on the back of another. It is lovely in

Wisdom Woman

WISDOM OF SOLOMON
7:22b-30

For she is a reflection of eternal light, a spotless mirror of the working of God. (7:26)

and life with her has no pain,
but gladness and joy.
[17] When I considered these things inwardly,
and pondered in my heart
that in kinship with wisdom
there is immortality,
[18] and in friendship with her, pure delight,
and in the labors of her hands, unfailing wealth,
and in the experience of her company,
understanding,
and renown in sharing her words,
I went about seeking how to get her for myself.
[19] As a child I was naturally gifted,
and a good soul fell to my lot;
[20] or rather, being good, I entered
an undefiled body.
[21] But I perceived that I would not possess
wisdom unless God gave her to me —
and it was a mark of insight to know
whose gift she was —
so I appealed to the Lord and implored him,
and with my whole heart I said:

9

"O God of my ancestors and Lord of mercy,
who have made all things by your word,
[2] and by your wisdom have formed humankind
to have dominion over the creatures
you have made,
[3] and rule the world in holiness
and righteousness,
and pronounce judgment in
uprightness of soul;
[4] give me the wisdom that sits by your throne,
and do not reject me from among
your servants.
[5] For I am your servant the son of
your serving girl,
a man who is weak and short-lived,
with little understanding of
judgment and laws;
[6] for even one who is perfect among
human beings
will be regarded as nothing without the
wisdom that comes from you.
[7] You have chosen me to be king of your people
and to be judge over your sons and daughters.
[8] You have given command to build a temple
on your holy mountain,
and an altar in the city of your habitation,
a copy of the holy tent that you prepared
from the beginning.
[9] With you is wisdom;

she who knows your works
and was present when you made the world;
she understands what is pleasing in your sight
and what is right according to
your commandments.
[10] Send her forth from the holy heavens,
and from the throne of your glory send her,
that she may labor at my side,
and that I may learn what is pleasing to you.
[11] For she knows and understands all things,
and she will guide me wisely in my actions
and guard me with her glory.
[12] Then my works will be acceptable,
and I shall judge your people justly,
and shall be worthy of the throne
of my father.
[13] For who can learn the counsel of God?
Or who can discern what the Lord wills?
[14] For the reasoning of mortals is worthless,
and our designs are likely to fail;

Gk. slave
Gk. throne

WISDOM WOMAN

THE ART OF THE SAINT JOHN'S BIBLE

³ But when an unrighteous man departed
    from her in his anger,
  he perished because in rage he
    killed his brother.
⁴ When the earth was flooded because of him,
    wisdom again saved it;
  steering the righteous man by a
    paltry piece of wood.

⁵ Wisdom also, when the nations in wicked
    agreement had been put to confusion,
  recognized the righteous man and preserved
    him blameless before God,
  and kept him strong in the face of his
    compassion for his child.

⁶ Wisdom rescued a righteous man when
    the ungodly were perishing;
  he escaped the fire that descended
    on the Five Cities.
⁷ Evidence of their wickedness still remains:
  a continually smoking wasteland;
  plants bearing fruit that does not ripen,
  and a pillar of salt standing as a monument
    to an unbelieving soul.
⁸ For because they passed wisdom by,
  they not only were hindered from
    recognizing the good,
  but also left for humankind a reminder
    of their folly,
  so that their failures could never go unnoticed.

⁹ Wisdom rescued from troubles
    those who served her.
¹⁰ When a righteous man fled from
    his brother's wrath,
  she guided him on straight paths;
  she showed him the kingdom of God,
  and gave him knowledge of holy things;
  she prospered him in his labors,
  and increased the fruit of his toil.
¹¹ When his oppressors were covetous,
  she stood by him and made him rich.
¹² She protected him from his enemies,
  and kept him safe from those who
    lay in wait for him;
  in his arduous contest she gave
    him the victory,
  so that he might learn that godliness is more
    powerful than anything else.

¹³ When a righteous man was sold, wisdom
    did not desert him,
  but delivered him from sin.

¹⁵ for a perishable body weighs down the soul,
  and the earthy tent burdens the
    thoughtful mind.
¹⁶ We can hardly guess at what is on earth,
  and what is at hand we find with labor;
  but who has traced out what is in the heavens?
¹⁷ Who has learned your counsel,
  unless you have given wisdom
  and sent your holy spirit from on high?
¹⁸ And thus the paths of those on
    earth were set right,
  and people were taught what pleases you,
  and were saved by wisdom."

10

Wisdom protected the first-formed father of the
    world, when he alone had been created;
  she delivered him from his transgression,
  and gave him strength to rule all things.

⁵ Or anxious
y. Gk
Gk She
ᵇ Or in Pentapolis
Gk she

how it unfolds from the center of the page when opened, but it increases the technical difficulty tenfold.

It is difficult to imagine a more perfect face for Wisdom. The crow's feet around her eyes and the sparkle in those eyes emit more joy than her slight smile suggests. Like Wisdom, she is full of light. She has squinted into the sun, and she has looked hard at life, and she has laughed. The lines on her forehead show she has worried and given her full attention to the task at hand. Her smile is knowing, somewhat secretive, but also intimate—she will tell us her secret if we ask.

The round frame of the mirror depicts the twenty-eight phases of the moon, another association with the feminine in the universe. In the four corners of the outer frame are paintings based on images from the Hubble telescope, again pointing to the cosmic nature of Wisdom. The shapes here, of the circle and the frame, hark back to the walled garden in Song of Solomon or look forward to the vision of Solomon's temple in Ezekiel. Fragments of the familiar, mirrored wisdom tree are again stamped along the border. When contemplating Wisdom, we should employ all our metaphors: journey, creation, reflection, and relationship, and any others that help us approach the mystery of God.

Over the course of the project each of the scribes made an error in the text that could not be erased. The only one who seemed to be immune was Brian Simpson. Finally here, in the last volume he did major work on as a scribe, he left out two lines. As usual when such things happened, the lines were striking in their importance! "I called on God, and the spirit of wisdom came to me." Donald Jackson decided that when lines were omitted they should be written in at the bottom and their place in the text acknowledged. In past volumes birds have most often "carried" the lines to their spot. This time, however, a bee was chosen to do the work. Sarah Harris and Donald Jackson worked out the design of the pulley system based on Leonardo da Vinci's mechanical drawings, and Chris Tomlin came in to paint this whimsical bee doing some heavy lifting.

Along the left margin is the second part of a text treatment by Sally Mae Joseph. It begins on the previous page with a reprise of the verse that was placed in Job and commissioned from one of the scribes, Angela Swan: "Wisdom is radiant and unfading and she is easily discerned by those who love her and is found by those who seek her." On this page the treatment traces a chain of thought called *sorites,* which connects a number of like statements. "The beginning of wisdom" is desire for instruction, which is love of Wisdom, which in turn causes one to obey her commands, thus bringing one closer to God and leading directly into the kingdom. What is required of us, therefore, is to seek, and if we are sincere we will no doubt end our journey in God's kingdom.

Creation, Covenant,
Shekinah, Kingdom

WISDOM OF SOLOMON
10–11
*Wisdom rescued from
troubles those who served her.
(10:9)*

*Although the text does not name the characters in
Israel's history under consideration, can you identify
and name them as you read along?*

The Wisdom of Solomon includes two chapters that re-
count the history of Wisdom from creation through the Israelites' stay in the desert. These chapters are the source for
the illumination on these pages, again celebrating Wisdom's
creative power and connection to human life. These chapters reference the major events in Genesis and Exodus. They
retell the history as though in an address to Wisdom, pointing out her constancy to humans. Adam, "the first-formed
father of the world," when he is outside the Garden of Eden,
is helped by Wisdom to gain dominion over the earth (Wis
10:1-2). Lot's wife remains a symbol of all of those who did
not trust in Wisdom, "a reminder of their folly" (Wis 10:8).
Wisdom is with Jacob in his toil and protects and prospers
him. She also goes with Joseph "into the dungeon" and gives
him power in the kingdom and honor (Wis 10:13-14).

It is understood that the people know these stories. They
are an important piece of the cultural memory, recorded in
Genesis and Exodus. The stories were passed down and appear in several forms in the Old Testament, including the
retelling of them in Psalms. This retelling, however, puts the

CREATION, COVENANT, SHEKINAH, KINGDOM

THE ART OF THE SAINT JOHN'S BIBLE

focus on Wisdom, God's "holy spirit" (with lower case) sent down and walking with us. For the people living in exile in Babylon, among foreign gods and the temples and courts of foreign rulers, a divine presence who knew their troubles and would guide them when the God of temple worship seemed far away was a source of sustenance and joy.

A list of possibilities for this illumination was given to Donald Jackson by the CIT. He devised a series of four panels that draws on illuminations of four passages in *Pentateuch* and *Prophets*. This illumination takes us back to the theme of creation running throughout *Wisdom Books*. Again, the focus is on Wisdom's presence at the beginning of time and throughout history, even to the end of the age. God's plan and Wisdom go hand in hand.

The four panels here bring to mind the four elements of the universe: earth, water, fire, and air. They refer back to the stories in the narrative: the Creation, the Flood, the Exodus, and the Promised Land.

The first two panels are most clearly tied to the creation theme. "She who knows your works and was present when you made the world," reads Wisdom 9:9. In the first panel the seven pieces from the *Creation* illumination are put in various widths, emphasizing the cycles of the moon that are associated with Wisdom, and the creation of humans, along

with the coral snake representing the Fall. The raven of the first panel (also seen in the Ecclesiastes frontispiece) is complemented by the dove in the second, an image of the spirit. The story of the Flood is a second creation story, as God again brings the world out of chaos and makes a covenant with Noah, gifting him the world and promising never again to wipe out creation by flood. "When the earth was flooded . . . Wisdom again saved it, steering the righteous man by a paltry piece of wood" reads Wisdom 10:4. It is in the connection between God and humanity that we see wisdom, the ingenuity of the ark.

Images of destruction, not just creation, also link the second and third panels to each other. The flash of color at the bottom of the second panel is a variation on the *Job Frontispiece*, imagery that continues into the next panel. In both cases, as with chaos in the first panel, destruction breaks the boundaries of the image, taking us beyond God's perfect plan. However, in the first frame the abundance of land and water also break the frame, and in the second the dove soars and lifts the olive branch outside of the margins. In the case of the flood, or of Israel in the desert, the chaos of humankind's disobedience exists alongside God's plan for salvation.

The third panel has the word "Shekinah" (The Hebrew pronunciation is "shuh-khee-**nuh**" although it is often pronounced by English speakers "shuh-**kayh**-nuh.") This is the English equivalent of the Hebrew word that describes God's presence or a symbol of God's presence on earth. The concept is found in Ezekiel when the presence of God leaves Jerusalem and the temple, but also earlier in Exodus to describe God dwelling in the tabernacle. The image is of the column of fire by which God led Israel out of Egypt. Again Wisdom was there: "She brought them over the Red Sea and led them through deep waters" (Wis 10:18). God appeared to Moses first in the burning bush and later to the people as fire on Mount Sinai. The people knew that God was present in the tabernacle because it glowed with the light of God's glory. The Hebrew word Shekinah itself is feminine, and it has been used by scholars to denote the feminine character of God, again a theme found throughout *Wisdom Books*. Izzy Pludwinski designed the word as it appears in gold in this illumination. Finally, it was in the Exodus that Israel became a nation, another act of creation.

The fourth panel takes a detail from the vision of Solomon's temple in Isaiah that focuses on the abundance provided to the people in the Promised Land and the eschatological meaning of the temple. Solomon, the invented speaker of the present book, sings the praises of Wisdom, who is with him, helping him to raise up a righteous kingdom. It is Solomon who built the first temple, and even after continued disobedience and the loss of the Promised Land there remains faith in God's mercy and knowledge that the temple will be restored. In God's return and the creation of the New Jerusalem, Wisdom is there. A number of verses in the passage apply here. Donald Jackson mentioned "She gave to holy people the reward of their labors" (Wis 10:17) as his inspiration. However, the following verse also applies to God's reconciling nature and the balance between creation and salvation history: "For you love all things that exist, and detest none of the things you have made . . . you spare all things, for they are yours, O LORD, you who love the living" (Wis 11:24, 26). Wisdom continually draws us to God and reveals God's mercy and promise.

Connecting these panels are batons and frames of gold and silver, wisdom and divinity, as we have seen from the first page of Job. These are not discrete events, but connected. Each of these moments in the history of Israel is one moment in the revelation of God's abiding presence with us. The words in the margin, "I was there," come from Proverbs 8:27, when Wisdom declares "I was there" at the moment of the creation. Donald Jackson sees this as a complementary notation to Isaiah's response to God, found in the margins of the *Vision of Isaiah* in *Prophets*, where he answers the call with the words, "Here am I."

◖ *Where do you perceive the presence of God in history and the world around you?*

This is the fourth text treatment in the volume by native Minnesotan Diane M. von Arx. The opening verse of the Rule of Benedict is "Listen carefully, my son, to the master's instructions, and attend to them with the ear of your heart." The command "Listen to him" was prominently treated in two places in the Gospel of Mark surrounding the account of the Transfiguration. The references to Saint John's Abbey are further deepened by two motifs running through the text treatment. At the center you will see the faint pattern of honeycomb, which is the pattern of the stained glass windows at both Saint John's and Saint Benedict's churches. Also running through the text are the voice-print images from *Psalms*. Those representations of the monks' song at prayer reflect the second directive of these verses, to sing hymns of praise to the Lord.

Diane M. von Arx's text treatments are marked by bold colors and strong images. In addition to this treatment in Sirach, she also contributed the dramatic *For I Know that My Redeemer Lives* (Job 19:25), *Send Out Your Bread upon the Waters* (Eccl 11:1), and *Faithful Friends* (Wis 6:14-22, located at Sir 7). Each of her treatments has a unique script and different color palette.

SIRACH 39:13-15

Let us look back at one other treatment by Diane M. von Arx, *Faithful Friends* (Sir 6:14-22). This passage picks up on themes in Proverbs and Ecclesiastes, and celebrates the good life enjoyed by those who seek wisdom. The wise appreciate the value of friendship and of discipline, and so are rooted and happy into old age. Their lives are built on a solid foundation, like the brick wall behind the calligraphy. Diane M. von Arx adds to this a reprise of the subtle honeycomb pattern. Like so many texts in *Wisdom Books*, this one is rich with metaphors: friends are a treasure and a saving medicine; Wisdom is good seed planted by those who toil in her garden; these laborers will harvest her fruits. For the undisciplined, however, wisdom is a heavy stone to be cast aside. This colorful treatment keeps the truth of good values before us, instructing us to cultivate wisdom and be disciplined. The result will be lasting friendships and peace in our relationships well into old age.

SIRACH 6:14-22

What images from Praise of Wisdom do you see in the illumination?

SIRACH 24

Come to me, you who desire me, and eat your fill of my fruits. (24:19)

The final illumination in Sirach is by Suzanne Moore. Her other illuminations include *Last Judgment* (Matt 24–25), *Calming the Storm* (Matt 8:23-27), *Choose Life* (Deut 30), and also *Yet You Did Not Return to Me* (Amos 4), which we will discuss later in this guide. Each is marked by bold swaths of arcing color. Unlike previous illuminations by this artist, however, this one is more representational. We can make out figures throughout.

The key motif here is fertility. It is everywhere, in the fruits and the wheat and in the female figure at the top right, with breasts and navel, that looks like an ancient totem of fertility. All things lead to and proceed from her, another evocation of Wisdom. As we see in the text, Wisdom invites: "Come to me, you who desire me, / and eat your fill of my fruits, / for the memory of me is sweeter than honey, / and the possession of me sweeter than honeycomb" (24:19-20). Comparing this illumination with *Last Judgment* and *Calming the Storm*, you will see that, as each moves from chaos to divinity, the image is marked by sweeping arcs and the same filigree stamp we see here. Compared to the illumination in Amos, the fertility symbol stands out in clear opposition to the devouring locust God sent to punish and draw back the Israelites. Platinum is used on the circles on both sides of the image.

This illumination also draws on the comparison made by Christian theologians between Christ and Wisdom. Jesus claims to be the bread of life and living water, and in this chapter Wisdom claims: "Those who eat of me will hunger for more, / and those who drink of me will thirst for more" (24:21). A taste of wisdom makes one want more, as insatiable as the desire between the lovers in the Song of Solomon. The fertility figure at the top of the page is also cruciform, making us think of the cross, and at the bottom is a round orange shape bisected that resembles previous images of eucharistic loaves of bread. The image on the

lower left appears to be a perfume bottle with an open mouth, from which rises a moonlike bubble. This image corresponds to verse 15: "Like cassia and camel's thorn I gave forth perfume, / and like choice myrrh I spread my fragrance." So beautiful are these two verses, in fact, of wisdom as honey and as perfume, that they are each given separate text treatments. Sirach 24:19-20 by Sally Mae Joseph appears in the margin at Sirach 13, and Sirach 24:12-17 weaves in and out of the text like vines in an elaborate treatment by Sue Hufton placed at Sirach 44–45.

Like Clay in the Hand of the Potter

SIRACH 33:13

LIKE CLAY IN THE HAND OF THE POTTER, TO BE MOLDED AS HE PLEASES, SO ALL ARE IN THE HAND OF THEIR MAKER, TO BE GIVEN WHATEVER HE DECIDES

This text treatment by Donald Jackson again picks up the themes of creation, distinctiveness, God's care, and growth through wisdom. It is God who has molded us and assigned us each our particular talents and quirks. Like a hand-fashioned work of pottery, each piece is unique and reflects its maker. The dynamic shape of the text and the subtle shifts of color speak to God's playfulness, making us "as he pleases" in all our diversity. None of us is perfect, but we are all special because God has made us. And God continues to mold us as we seek wisdom and grow. The text itself conforms to the shape of a hand cupping rotating clay. Finally, as a potter puts a mark on a finished work, so this text treatment ends with a gold stamp, or mark, as if God had pressed God's thumb to the page.

SIRACH 33:13

A carpet page closes the volume of *Wisdom Books*. We call it a carpet page because it fills the white space left at the end of the volume and consists of a lightly printed pattern rather than elaborate and heavy illumination. However, this is more of a stand-alone piece than other carpet pages, a text treatment and image. The second function of a carpet page, to distract and diminish the show-through of a heavy illumination on the other side of the skin, is not necessary here at the end of a volume. It is more intentionally decorative. The stamp made from the mirrored cloth we saw most prominently in *Seven Pillars of Wisdom* is used again here, in colors we recognize from the garden in the Song of Solomon. The fragments from the garden are also mixed in to give more structure to the tree. The wisdom tree can be

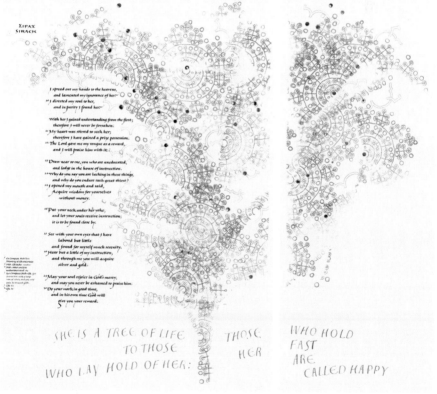

SIRACH CARPET PAGE

compared to the tree of life carpet page at the end of the Gospel of Luke, which was also based in part on textile patterns. It reminds us, too, of how much nature there has been in this volume: trees, birds, lilies, fish, and butterflies fluttering at the margins. Trees weave the natural world into the text, filling it with images of beauty, complexity, and fruitfulness. We leave the wisdom books with one final aphorism. We should hold onto wisdom as we embrace life. In holding to wisdom we will find happiness. In these books we have taken up some of the heavy and dark issues of human existence: suffering, injustice, exile, longing, and death. In the end we are encouraged to live, to experience beauty, and always to seek God and God's partner in creation, Wisdom.

❡ *If you were going to take with you a few "words of wisdom" from these books, what would they be? How will you carry these words with you?*

PROPHETS

A CONTEMPORARY picture of a prophet is almost always of some-one foretelling a coming doomsday. Prophets stand in city parks or on street corners, looking disillusioned and marginal, living portraits of the "signs of the times," and invariably, their conclusions are dismal. We also associate prophecy with seeing the future. Prophets tell us what will happen, again usually in a negative context. So we might hear the media describe scientists raising a warning about global warming or a flu epidemic, or economists predicting the collapse of a currency or economy as "doomsday prophets." If they let loose with a particularly vehement rant, it might be called a "jeremiad," after the prophet Jeremiah's dark messages. If you page through *Prophets,* you will certainly see some dark and frightening images. However, you will also be met by rainbows—glorious rays of color filling up some of the illuminations. Where did those come from?

The truth is, the prophetic literature of the Old Testament is about hope as well as destruction. The prophets were not trying to cast down the people, but to lift up and sustain them in a time of trouble. They were calling the people to live better, to make a perfect society, to return to right worship of God, and in times of pain and exile to realize that God was still calling them and waiting to take them back, and in fact had a plan for them and for all nations. The hope at the center of the prophecies is the messiah, the one who would come to restore God's kingdom on earth. For Christians, these messianic prophecies point to Jesus Christ.

The basic comparison between the prophets of the Old Testament and some modern-day self-styled prophets holds. They did bring a basic message that unless the people turned to God they would face exile, collapse, and ruin. What is different, however, is that the call of the Old Testament prophets is not personal, not made to individuals accused of sin in an effort to turn their lives around, but is collective. The call is for the nation of Israel to return to God in right worship and to build a society based on justice and compassion. The salvation is for the whole people, the promise of a king whose kingdom will be eternal, a Prince of Peace, Wonderful Counselor, Everlasting Father, Emmanuel. The vision is larger than the recruitment of individuals to a personal relationship with Jesus. It is a vision of God's plan through all time, the transformation of the world.

The Old Testament prophets are primarily concerned not with the future, but with the present. They live and speak during a time of great upheaval and pain. The Israelites lost the Promised Land, their kingdoms fell, and even the temple was destroyed. They were carried off in bondage and exile, their religion crushed and their society dismantled. They looked to the prophets for answers about what had befallen them. How could this have happened to God's chosen people?

One explanation offered by the prophets is that the people have, through years of disobedience and idol worship, driven God from the sanctuary. Some prophets see the fall and exile as God's punishment for breaking the commandments, particularly the first commandment not to worship idols. In any event, the prophecies never end in judgment, but always proceed to the promise of God's love and mercy and desire for Israel's return. The description of God's wrath and punishment is always followed by the promise of forgiveness and the establishment of a new and perfect kingdom.

When Donald Jackson presented this volume to the Committee on Illumination and Text (CIT) at the Hill Museum & Manuscript Library at Saint John's University, he lovingly paused over pages of solid text. It is tempting to jump from illumination to illumination, as we are sometimes tempted to jump to the more entertaining or better-known passages in the Bible itself. Stopping at a set of columns on the page, however, Donald will say: "Look at the nobility there." What he is seeing is the calligraphy, the heart of the project and the heart of his art, the letters on the page, making words, making lines of words. It is about a steady and even hand in every sense. It is about balance and order, white spaces and inked figures.

On these pages your eye might be drawn to the shift between the lighter italic of the poetry and the solid prose text. Consider the care and attention that goes into these two forms, put on the page by different artists as they create a page. Also consider the themes emphasized by *The Saint John's Bible*. In this volume you will see the theme of transformation again and again, in the calls to the prophets and the appeals they make to the people. You will also see the theme of justice for God's people. What is it God has called the people to become? If God is to return and dwell with them again, what kind of place does God require for a dwelling? What kind of people can show God to the world?

How does this illumination meet your expectations for the opening of Prophets?

Prophets begins with what Donald Jackson has called a "reverse carpet page," because it is found here at the beginning of the book instead of at the end. Past volumes of *The Saint John's Bible* have started with a full-page illumination (each of the gospels, Acts, Genesis, Psalms, Job, Ecclesiastes). This book, however, begins quietly, introducing two thematic elements that will be important in the whole volume, the seraphs' wings and the temple path grid.

As we have just said, carpet pages are usually found at the end of individual books, as a rest for the eye and as a

Isaiah Reverse Carpet Page

ISAIAH 1

The vision of Isaiah son of Amoz, which he saw concerning Judah and Jerusalem. (1:1)

ISAIAH 2:4

screen against any show-through from a heavy illumination on the other side of the vellum page. This page has the same simplicity and light color scheme as a carpet page, and in fact some of the individual prophetic books in the volume (Amos, Haggai, Zechariah) will end with a repetition of the motif in whatever space is available after the text. In a larger way, however, this piece opens and closes *Prophets*, enclosing it and perhaps attempting to contain it.

The image refers to a major theme in the prophetic literature. The seraph wings most obviously allude to God's messengers and more particularly to God's direct interaction with the prophets. These messages and messengers, however, are part of a larger focus in the volume on transformation. The prophets are called to dramatic service to God, and they also call on the people of Israel to change their ways and transform their society in order to renew and maintain their covenant with God. The grid echoes the path of Ezekiel through the vision of the temple and so reflects the journey of the prophet and of the people of Israel, a journey of exile and return, as they seek out the ways of God.

Finally, above the book title and *incipit* for Isaiah are five lamps. The first column of text is further punctuated by three sets of five gold blocks. The gold blocks, in the opening page and throughout *The Saint John's Bible*, reveal the presence of God. They are sometimes placed randomly, as on the previous page, to suggest that God is present throughout the world of human action. At other times these blocks (and sometimes bars) are used to draw together and make more orderly the other, more chaotic elements of an illumination. In the first column of text in Isaiah the lamps and squares add a sense of royalty, an elevated nobility. Several of the prophetic visions describe God on a throne, represented in the illuminations as a larger block of gold. The image of God as king was important to Israel during this time of siege and collapse. This opening of the prophetic books is a reflection of what lies within—transformation, journey, and also the unfolding of the story of God as king and what lies ahead, God as messiah and savior.

THE ART OF THE SAINT JOHN'S BIBLE

Justice for God's people, and the importance of creating a just society, is another major theme emphasized by the text treatments and illuminations in *The Saint John's Bible*. It appears here in two text treatments for Isaiah 1 and 2 by Sally Mae Joseph. Again, it is important that we pay attention to the words of the prophets and the portrait they paint of a hopeful future. The call is to "seek justice" and work on behalf of the oppressed and vulnerable. The words of Isaiah 2:4 have been repeated as a slogan and in fact engraved on monuments for peace throughout the ages. The great African American spiritual "Down by the Riverside" used this verse in its jubilant refrain: "Ain't gonna study war no more." This verse was picked up by the peace movement of the 1960s and '70s, and is sung today by scouts around the campfire.

Turning swords of war into plowshares for growing food is a powerful image. It is so central that it is repeated again in Micah 4:3. The vision of God's perfect kingdom is first of all one where there is no war. As set down in the opening of the Bible, the creation in Genesis, God's vision is for fruitfulness, for growth and renewal and peace. Interestingly, both these text treatments use the word "Learn":
"Learn to do good," and then "Neither shall they learn war any more." In the fallen world, living up to God's purpose is hard work, and it is a process. We have to study and learn it, turning our attention to it.

ISAIAH 1:16-17 AND 2:4
They shall beat their swords into plowshares. (2:4)

He shall judge
between the nations
and shall arbitrate
for many peoples

they shall beat their
swords into plowshares
and their spears
into pruning hooks

·NATION·SHALL·NOT·LIFT·UP·
·SWORD·AGAINST·NATION·
·NEITHER·SHALL·THEY·
·LEARN·WAR·ANY·MORE·

ISAIAH 2:4

Vision of Isaiah

ISAIAH 6
I saw the Lord sitting on a throne, high and lofty; and the hem of his robe filled the temple. (6:1)

What elements of Isaiah's vision do you see in the illumination?

The book of Isaiah begins with a series of prophetic messages. God speaks first. In the poetry we hear God's sorrow and disappointment, frustration and anger at the people. We hear the call to return, to follow and learn the ways of God, and the promise of God's glory. It is not until chapter 6 that the book backs up and gives us the story of the call of Isaiah, the subject of the first major illumination.

The call of Isaiah is a royal and frightening vision. It frightens him because, as he says, he is unclean and living among unclean people. He recognizes that the people of Israel have not lived up to God's desires for them. He also surely knows the part of the Torah that says no one can see God directly and live. As a Jew in this period he would be concerned with purification and holiness—only the priests who had a certain level of ritual purity could approach God in the temple, and only the high priest could enter the holy of holies where the presence of the Lord dwelled in the ark. For God to appear to him surrounded by seraphim would be for the very essence of holiness to mix with the impure—a dangerous combination in the Old Testament. However, one of the seraphim comes to him with a burning ember and purifies his lips. He will not just see God; he will carry God's message to the people.

The figure of Isaiah is sprawled across the bottom of the center panel. He is naked, vulnerable, human, and yet also seems held by seraph wings. You can see the red ember held to his mouth by long gold tongs, also extending from a seraph's wing. This is the only mention of seraphim in the Old Testament, although some scholars have linked them to the fiery serpents in the book of Numbers. Their name comes from the Hebrew word for fire, and because of this passage Christianity associates them with the fire and light of both purification and God's glory.

To make this image, Donald Jackson first went in search of images of wings from the time of the Babylonian exile. These wings come from images found on Assyrian reliefs at the British Museum. Jackson wanted to find images for all

THE ART OF THE SAINT JOHN'S BIBLE

the strange visions of the prophets that might reflect the imagery of the world they lived in. As our dreams are often made of the stuff we see around us in our waking life, Jackson believed the prophetic visions were informed by the images—strange to us but everyday to them—adorning the temples and public buildings of the Assyrian and Babylonian world of the exile. Once he found the images of wings from the period, Jackson took them and manipulated them on the computer until they had the twisted, active shapes he wanted. He converted these to stamps that are used throughout the volume.

It is also said that the seraphim are "in attendance" on the king (6:2). Ultimately, the core of this image is the figure of God as king. The image consists of three arches and is further framed by ten lamp stands. The smoking lamps add to the atmospheric interior, perhaps suggesting the smell of burning oil or sacrificial incense. Fragments of a palace wall run through it. Purple, for royalty, is the dominant color of the piece. The red cloth pieces are the hems of the garment that Isaiah sees filling the temple. Temple and royal court are thus combined in this vision. The throne itself is a box of gold framing a human figure's head and shoulders. It is similar to a piece of the shaft of gold we saw in the frontispiece for the Gospel of Luke, *Birth of Christ,* where the image of God was a gold shaft emanating from a stylized, throne-like manger.

Also introduced in this piece are blocks of rainbow colors. This motif will run throughout the book, joining gold as a sign of divine presence. The image comes from Ezekiel 1:28, where Ezekiel says: "Like the bow in a cloud on a rainy day, such was the appearance of the splendor all around. This was the appearance of the likeness of the glory of the Lord." Again, it is the glory that is emphasized. Of course, rainbows always connect us with the Genesis account of Noah and God's first covenant not to destroy the people. The ongoing nature of this promise is ever more important as the people find themselves under siege, overthrown, and marched off to exile, their cities and even the temple destroyed.

It is from this passage that we get the "Holy, Holy," the song of the angels. This hymn, sung by most Christian denominations during their eucharistic prayer, is also called the *Sanctus,* the Latin word for "Holy." It is one of the earliest pieces of Christian liturgy, appearing throughout the Christian world in the late third and early fourth centuries. In the illumination you will see it three times in three languages: Hebrew at the top left, Greek in the center, and Latin at the right.

This actually represents yet another major theme in *The Saint John's Bible,* attention to Christian prayer and worship. Because this is a Bible commissioned by a community of Benedictine monks, the parts of Scripture that surface in the liturgy get special attention. The *Sanctus* makes an early connection by Christians back to Old Testament texts, and in fact

VISION OF ISAIAH

THE ART OF THE SAINT JOHN'S BIBLE

Isaiah is quoted more often in the New Testament than any other book but Psalms. Christians looked to the prophets for answers to what was happening in their own time. For this reason you will see attention to many passages that foretell the coming of a messiah whom Christians identify as Jesus.

Finally, in the margin we see Isaiah's response to God's call. After the seraph has cleansed his lips with the burning ember, he answers: "Here am I: Send me!" When he leaves this temple it will be as God's prophet with a message for the people, who also need to be cleansed and made holy.

◗ *As you contemplate this page, speak aloud the marginal words: "Here am I: Send me!" What is God calling you to do? Who is God calling you to be?*

What do the names in this illumination tell us about the Messiah?

This full-page illumination is by Thomas Ingmire, who also did the illuminations for *Ten Commandments* (Exod 20), *Beatitudes* (Matt 5:3-12), and *I AM Sayings* (John 6–15). We made reference to this illumination when discussing his dramatic treatments at the end of Job.

The passage in Isaiah is familiar to many people from Handel's great work, *The Messiah*. Sung often at Christmas, it is crowned by the great Hallelujah chorus. This illumination is likewise crowned with Hallelujahs! You can almost see the trumpets raised and blasting with the announcement. Also here are echoes of the rainbow motif, not in color but in shape. The names of God are written on the bows: "Prince of Peace," "King of Kings," "Everlasting Father," "Immanuel," and the announcement: "For unto us a child is born" and "God is with us."

In addition to the bows and the words of this piece, there is the intricate geometric gold stamp we have seen in many other illuminations. It sparkles and shines here like the stars or the sun or even bursts of fireworks. This is truly an illumination of celebration.

The image of a birth foretold is indeed a glorious one. If you read the whole of chapters 8–11 you will see that they primarily foretell the destruction of the disobedient and unfaithful people. But these dark predictions are balanced by hope. Again, the prophet's messages contain the promise of God's ultimate plan for the people, one of reconciliation, of communion with God, and not of abandonment and destruction. And it is a message for all the nations, as seen in chapter 11, not just the remnant of Israel. Every Christmas season Christians celebrate with the same sense of wonder and anticipation of God's promises.

Donald Jackson has said of this page, "it is truly a living thing." In its original the inks and gold leaf do seem to make the letters dance. Everything stands out clearly and distinctly, and the page has depth and, well, movement. Especially wonderful is to think of turning to it in a book, watching the words lift and rise, then fold out of sight.

ישעיה

HALLELUJAH

THEREFORE THE LORD HIMSELF WILL GIVE YOU A SIGN LOOK THE YOUNG WOMAN IS WITH CHILD AND SHALL BEAR A SON AND SHALL NAME HIM IMMANUEL

MESSIANIC PREDICTIONS

Insect Marginalia

SCARAB

At Isaiah 30 we encounter the first of five insect illustrations by Chris Tomlin for the margins of *Prophets*. You have probably noticed the butterflies and dragonflies by nature illustrator Tomlin in earlier volumes. In *Prophets*, however, less celebrated insects take center stage. The first is a scarab, a very important insect in antiquity. In ancient Egypt the scarab was as symbolically sacred as the cross is to Christians. Scarabs permeated the culture, as amulets and ornaments and as seals. Made out of clay, a scarab would be inscribed on the flat or abdomen side with names, mottos, or other patterns, and glazed in dark blues and greens. There is clear evidence that the scarab spread beyond Egypt's borders, and many have been found in Palestine, the Near East, Spain, Italy, Greece, and elsewhere.

Often the images in the margins are purely for decoration, but in this case it does amplify the text of Isaiah 30:1-5. These verses scold the Israelites for going to seek shelter from their enemies in Egypt instead of trusting God to deliver them. Any association with Egypt, given that the primary story of the people of Israel is their deliverance from Egypt under Moses and Aaron, is a grave turning away from God. The close ties gained from living for generations, albeit under slavery, in Egypt, must have remained a great temptation for the people. After all, in the wilderness they spent a lot of time grumbling that things were better in Egypt, where at least there were resources.

The major claim against the Israelites is that they turned and worshiped other gods. To turn to the amulets of Egypt for protection, instead of to God, would indeed, as the passage reads, become their shame and disgrace (Isa 30:3, 5). The scarab was used as a seal in much the same way as we use rubber stamps today to impress something with an image. This is another resonance with the work of Donald Jackson, who has very frequently employed stamps in the illuminations of *The Saint John's Bible*.

In the margins at Jeremiah 17 we find an illustration of two black crickets. These field crickets are plentiful in Minnesota, the home of Saint John's Abbey. They are also

THE ART OF THE SAINT JOHN'S BIBLE

closely related to the more voracious and mobile locusts we read about in the Old Testament, particularly in connection with plagues. Locusts are not only found in the plagues against Egypt in Exodus, but also in many of the prophets, including Isaiah, here in Jeremiah, and in Joel, Amos, and Nahum. At Jeremiah 35 is another loud insect that can be heard in central Minnesota. The whine of the cicada is a sign of summer.

The final insect in the margins by Chris Tomlin is found at Ezekiel 22. This insect has particular resonance for Saint John's Abbey and Minnesota. It is the dreaded black fly! Although mostly just a nuisance, black flies are related to mosquitoes, and the females get their sustenance from blood. The bite of a black fly is more painful than a mosquito's and brings up an alarming welt. In the northern regions, particularly in the lakes and woods close to the Canadian border, the swarms of black flies can be intense and, indeed, plague-like. The lakes of Minnesota and Canada are a perfect breeding ground for the noxious insect.

TWO FIELD CRICKETS

Extending the
Prophet's Call

ISAIAH 40 AND 49

A text treatment of Isaiah 40:1-5 complements the text treatments at the opening of the book of Isaiah and extends the messianic nature of Isaiah's prophecies. Isaiah 40 marks a major shift in the book of Isaiah. The rest of the

ISAIAH 49:1-4

66

book is called "Second Isaiah" because it was written long after Isaiah 1–39 by a separate author. There are references showing that the exile is officially over and the people can return from Babylon. The end of exile and return to Jerusalem is in fact heralded like a new Exodus—God delivering the people from bondage. This word of comfort lets the people know that their suffering is at an end, and also urges them to participate in the return. It is an announcement of the beginning of a new age for Israel, a call to return and to build God's kingdom of justice and right worship in Jerusalem.

The "one who cries out in the wilderness" is identified by Christians as John the Baptist. Isaiah 40:3 is quoted in each of the four gospels to introduce John (Matt 3:1, Mark 1:3, Luke 3:4-6, and John 1:23). In Matthew 17:13 the correspondence is deepened when Jesus tells the disciples that Elijah has already returned to prepare the way, and they know he is talking about John the Baptist. The message the Baptist brings is the beginning of the reign of God, the transformation of society according to God's plan.

A second text treatment, Isaiah 49:1-4, *Listen to Me, O Coastlands*, draws attention to the universalism so evident in Isaiah. The prophet is calling to those nations and peoples outside Israel. He is proclaiming a vision of God's kingdom on earth that includes the Gentiles, another theme that is important to early Christian communities. This reading is also associated with John the Baptist. It is from the first reading during the Liturgy of the Word for the feast of St. John the Baptist, June 24. As the patron saint of Saint John's Abbey and Abbey Church, John the Baptist is celebrated particularly by the monks. The verse also resonates with the Rule of Benedict, whose first word is "Listen." Texts that call us to listen are important to Benedictines. The ink used for this treatment and others in *Prophets* came from a family firm in Japan. You will notice the variation in the color here, another way that the materials often affect the result of the calligraphy.

Suffering Servant

ISAIAH 52–53
Surely he has borne our iniquities and carried our diseases. (53:4)

What does this illumination have to say about human suffering and its relationship to God?

One of the more alarming illuminations is that of the *Suffering Servant*. The passage is important to both Jews and Christians. In the Jewish tradition, the suffering servant is often identified with the people Israel, the prophet himself, or someone who fits the context of the time the book was written. The portrayal of the Suffering Servant is significant because it shows a positive purpose for suffering. This is contrary to the biblical tradition that sees suffering as punishment.

Christians, of course, see the Suffering Servant as a vision of Christ, whose redemptive suffering is central to the Christian faith. Particularly following the *Messianic Predictions*, it is jarring to be brought back into the world of death and human suffering by this passage. These two illuminations together, however, bring out the true nature of Christ. Though he was God, he became one of us. Though he was the king of kings, he identified with us completely in our suffering.

This meditation on human suffering brings together many types of pain and oppression in the world today. There is the chain-link fence familiar from refugee camps and wartime prisons, to anyone who has been separated and barred from entry. This image was taken from pictures of the fence around Guantanamo Bay, Cuba. Closer to the figure the confinement is still more oppressive, suggestive of prison bars. It even suggests the narrow bars of the Door of No Return at Elmina Castle in Ghana, the passage through which Africans were taken onto ships, bound for slavery in the New World. This association is also echoed by the figure itself. Drawn from images of starving children, victims of the African famines, it is a familiar portrait of suffering, and one that never ceases to move us. Oppression, injustice, neglect, war, and poverty are indeed the result of our iniquity. Here stands a figure that is vulnerable and yet able to redeem us.

At the base of the illumination is a lamb on a field of red and purple. As the biblical passage reminds us, this is the story of our sacrificial lamb, the one "like a lamb that is led to the slaughter." The crucifixion accounts in the four gospels also draw attention to the silence of Jesus as he is led from his arrest and before his accusers in the following days. Above the figure is a cross, also constructed of bars, but this time bars of light. The distance between the Suffering Servant and the cross of gold is traversed by red and purple, again the colors of blood sacrifice but also of royal promise.

❧ *How does this illumination work against or with the Messianic Predictions in telling the story of Christ?*

SUFFERING SERVANT

Annotation

Turn the page from the Suffering Servant, and you will see a highlighted text, Isaiah 55:1-3. The CIT asked Donald Jackson if he could find a way to draw attention to this text, visually highlight it in some way. In the end, Jackson decided it should be simply underlined, as a way to draw the eye but also in a way that "annotates" the text as many people annotate important texts. Many read the Bible with a pen in hand, and even a notebook. It is almost impossible to read the text without being moved, or wanting to preserve some piece of it in your mind and heart. For centuries, readers have left their mark on books by writing notes in the margin or simply underlining passages they want to return to.

This passage is particularly soothing after a contemplation of the Suffering Servant illumination. "Ho, everyone who thirsts, come to the waters; and you that have no money, come, buy and eat!" (55:1). Again, there are parallels to John's portrayal of Jesus as the living water and to the eucharistic meal. However, on an even more basic level this is a call for everyone who is suffering to come and be satisfied. Again it draws attention to God's concern for the poor and suffering, and God's desire to meet these needs. This annotation also draws our attention to another important word, "listen." With this slight nod to the Rule of Benedict and acknowledgment that the pages of poetry here are constantly shifting and full of promise, we hear again the command to pay attention to the word of God, to "listen to God and live."

Ho, everyone who thirsts,
  come to the waters;
and you that have no money,
  come, buy and eat!
Come, buy wine and milk
  without money and without price.
² Why do you spend your money for
    that which is not bread,
  and your labor for that which does not satisfy?
Listen carefully to me, and eat what is good,

ISAIAH 55:1–2

THE ART OF THE SAINT JOHN'S BIBLE

ISAIAH 60:1-3

This text treatment by Sally Mae Joseph seems to complete the cycle from birth through suffering to resurrection. It is another messianic prediction, declaring that the light of the world will come to all peoples. In addition to the text itself, these two pages are strewn with small gold points of divine light, encouraging us to read all the good news in chapters 60–62. The red chapter heads also link the chapters and further tie them to the color of the text treatment. In the beginning was light, and light has been a constant throughout the Scriptures. The continuing work of creation is celebrated in the renewing light of this passage.

Chapter 61 begins with another well-known verse: "[The LORD] has sent me to bring good news to the oppressed, to bind up the brokenhearted, to proclaim liberty to the captives, and release to the prisoners" (61:1). Liberation from exile is another opportunity to be made anew, to create the kingdom God has had in mind from the beginning.

Gold leaf, at the center of illumination, reflects light throughout *The Saint John's Bible*. The light shines in the frontispiece of Luke's gospel, where the birth of the Savior is portrayed as a shaft of gold light that illuminates the human observers. We saw this divine light also in *Wisdom Books*, where wisdom reflects God's glory as in a mirror.

Chapter 62 repeats the theme of light: "For Zion's sake I will not keep silent, and for Jerusalem's sake I will not rest, until her vindication shines out like the dawn, and her salvation like a burning torch" (62:1). This light is apparent in the haloes behind the heads of the disciples in Acts 5, the illumination of the early Christian community. God continuously brings light into the world and invites us to shine.

THE ART OF THE SAINT JOHN'S BIBLE

This text treatment by Thomas Ingmire has more in common with the text treatments in *Wisdom Books* than the others in *Prophets*. The text speaks of Jerusalem as a woman: "I will extend prosperity to her like a river, and the wealth of the nations like an overflowing stream; and you shall nurse and be carried on her arm, and dandled on her knees." However, the verse shifts here, and suddenly not Jerusalem but God is compared to a mother: "As a mother comforts her child, so I will comfort you; you shall be comforted in Jerusalem."

It is a complex analogy, and up-lifting in the extreme to the people in exile: Jerusalem will once again be a comfort and source of nurture to her people. She will be the place where the people will be nurtured and comforted by Mother God. This feminine nature of God is explored in more depth in *Wisdom Books*, where Wisdom becomes the archetypal image of the feminine presence of the divine.

As a Mother Comforts Her Child

ISAIAH 66:12-13

ISAIAH 66:12-13

How does the call of Jeremiah differ from the call of Isaiah?

JEREMIAH 1:1-19
I appointed you a prophet to the nations. (1:5c)

There are some key differences between the account of Jeremiah's calling and Isaiah's vision. The encounter here more closely resembles the relationship between parent and child. The Lord speaks directly to Jeremiah, beginning not with a command but with a statement of love and creation: "Before I formed you in the womb I knew you, and before you were born I consecrated you." Isaiah also expresses this conviction, and it is a source of comfort as well as authority. Jeremiah has been lovingly created and chosen by God.

Like Isaiah, Jeremiah responds by speaking of his own unworthiness. How can he speak for God when he is only a boy, even a specially chosen son of God? Again God is gentle with Jeremiah. Like a parent speaking to a child, God says: "Do not say, 'I am only a boy,'" and then "Do not be afraid of them, for I am with you to deliver you." Finally, God touches Jeremiah, putting his words directly into Jeremiah's mouth. In contrast to the vision of fiery seraphim with embers, God touches Jeremiah. Rather than burning his mouth with an ember, this touch seems to us readers reassuring and nurturing. God proceeds to teach Jeremiah how to prophesy, again beginning with a question: "Jeremiah, what do you see?"

This is another strange start. The word "jeremiad" has come down through the language from this prophet because of his fiery laments. A jeremiad is a doomsday prediction or excessive outpouring of grief and anger. The message that comes out of Jeremiah's mouth will be one of fiery destruction.

He will also, here and in the short book of Lamentations that follows, give expression to Israel's complaints, even against God, as they pour out their own grief and frustration to God over their suffering and feelings of abandonment. Similar poems called laments are also found in Psalms. Always Jeremiah's predictions are tempered by God's promise that if the people return to worship, change

74

ירמיה

The words of Jeremiah son of Hilkiah, of the priests who were in Anathoth in the land of Benjamin, to whom the word of the LORD came in the days of King Josiah son of Amon of Judah, in the thirteenth year of his reign. It came also in the days of King Jehoiakim son of Josiah of Judah, and until the end of the eleventh year of King Zedekiah son of Josiah of Judah, until the captivity of Jerusalem in the fifth month. ¶ Now the word of the LORD came to me saying,

⁵ "Before I formed you in the womb I knew you,
 and before you were born I consecrated you;
 I appointed you a prophet to the nations."

⁶ Then I said, "Ah, Lord GOD! Truly I do not know how to speak, for I am only a boy." ⁷ But the LORD said to me,

 "Do not say, 'I am only a boy';
 for you shall go to all to whom I send you,
 and you shall speak whatever I command you.

⁸ Do not be afraid of them,
 for I am with you to deliver you,
 says the LORD."

⁹ Then the LORD put out his hand and touched my mouth; and the LORD said to me,

 "Now I have put my words in your mouth.

¹⁰ See, today I appoint you over nations
 and over kingdoms,
 to pluck up and to pull down,
 to destroy and to overthrow,
 to build and to plant."

¹¹ ¶ The word of the LORD came to me, saying, "Jeremiah, what do you see?" And I said, "I see a branch of an almond tree." ¹² Then the LORD said to me, "You have seen well, for I am watching over my word to perform it." ¹³ The word of the LORD came to me a second time, saying, "What do you see?" And I said, "I see a boiling pot, tilted away from the north." ¶ Then the LORD said to me: Out of the north disaster shall break out on all the inhabitants of the land. ¹⁴ For now I am calling all the tribes of the kingdoms of the north, says the LORD; and they shall come and all of them shall set their thrones at the entrance of

the gates of Jerusalem, against all its surrounding walls and against all the cities of Judah. And I will utter my judgements against them, for all their wickedness in forsaking me; they have made offerings to other gods, and worshiped the works of their own hands. But you, gird up your loins; stand up and tell them everything that I command you. Do not break down before them, or I will break you before them. ¹⁸ And I for my part have made you today a fortified city, an iron pillar, and a bronze wall, against the whole land—against the kings of Judah, its princes, its priests, and the people of the land. ¹⁹ They will fight against you; but they shall not prevail against you, for I am with you, says the LORD, to deliver you.

The word of the LORD came to me, saying, "Go and proclaim in the hearing of Jerusalem, Thus says the LORD:

 I remember the devotion of your youth,
 your love as a bride,
 how you followed me in the wilderness,
 in a land not sown.

³ Israel was holy to the LORD,
 the first fruits of his harvest.
 All who ate of it were held guilty;
 disaster came upon them,
 says the LORD.

⁴ ¶ Hear the word of the LORD, O house of Jacob, and all the families of the house of Israel. ⁵ Thus says the LORD:

 What wrong did your ancestors find in me
 that they went far from me,
 and went after worthless things, and became
 worthless themselves?

⁶ They did not say, "Where is the LORD
 who brought us up from the land of Egypt,
 who led us in the wilderness,
 in a land of deserts and pits,
 in a land of drought and deep darkness,
 in a land that no one passes through,
 where no one lives?"

⁷ I brought you into a plentiful land
 to eat its fruits and its good things.
 But when you entered you defiled my land,
 and made my heritage an abomination.

⁸ The priests did not say, "Where is the LORD?"
 Those who handle the law did not know me;
 the rulers transgressed against me;
 the prophets prophesied by Baal,
 and went after things that do not profit.

JEREMIAH FRONTISPIECE

their ways, and follow God, they will be redeemed and the covenant restored. However, Jeremiah's work as a prophet will be hard and unfruitful. God tells him at the very outset that he will speak, but no one will listen. Maybe this is why God is so gentle with Jeremiah, promising him that he has been with him before he was born and is there with him like a parent with a child.

Turning to the opening of Jeremiah, you might or might

PROPHETS

not be struck by the complexity of the page. One of the biggest challenges of *Prophets* for the team in Wales was the constant shifting between prose and poetry. These pages certainly demonstrate that challenge. In fact, one of the first decisions about the style of the book was not to use elaborate capitals at the beginning of each chapter. The capitals had been a hallmark of *Pentateuch* and *Gospels and Acts*, but would not work in *Prophets*. The primary reason was the number of chapters that begin with poetry. The poetry is in a different, lighter script closer to italic, and also needs to be spaced carefully to meet the standards for use of the New Revised Standard Version. Instead of elaborate initial capitals, Donald Jackson decided the focus would be on the chapter numbers; there are 219 colored boxes with gold numerals in this volume.

On the two-page spread that ends the book of Isaiah and opens the book of Jeremiah, you are looking at the work of seven artists. Donald Jackson did the book title for Jeremiah as he did the book titles for all the other prophetic books. The challenge was to manage the scale of the boxes and text so that one that held the name of Jeremiah and Zechariah looked consistent with the shorter names of Joel, Amos, and Hosea. The Hebrew name of the book, "Isaiah" in the left-hand margin, and "Jeremiah" above the book title, were done by Izzy Pludwinski, who did all the Hebrew lettering. Sue Hufton, meanwhile, did the English text for all the running heads. Sally Mae Joseph did the text treatment of the call of Jeremiah, and also the italic text, in other words the lighter-weight poetry on the two pages. She was working in spaces left on the ruled page by Susan Leiper, who was the scribe for the heavier prose text of the passage. Finally, Brian Simpson wrote the capital in gold in the blue box for chapter 2 when he went through and added all the chapter numbers. Of course, no artist could approach the pages before the hide had been scrutched and sanded, dried and prepared. Once the skin was ready, Sarah Harris, who was then the studio assistant but has since been made studio manager, carefully ruled it with lines that are scarcely visible even on the vellum.

THE ART OF THE SAINT JOHN'S BIBLE

When Donald Jackson pages through the originals he is likely to stop at a page like the spread at Jeremiah 28–30. "Look at that," he remarks, "the nobility of those columns and that text." What he is seeing and admiring is the calligraphy itself. What he sees is the beauty of what can only be called "a steady hand." Although he says he can pick out the subtle variations that mark the hand of each of the scribes, the continuity of the text is what stands out to the more casual reader. Jackson is the one who invented this script, designed to carry the gravity of God's word but also be pleasing and legible to the modern eye. As the scribes have fallen into a rhythm and mastered the script over the years, the calligraphy has become more confident, more natural, and more sure. Still, Donald Jackson can identify the work of any particular scribe by looking at the page. Variation in the tail of a *p* or *f* or a slight flourish of a *y* or *g* will give them away. A book like *Prophets*, with pages of poetry and also the columns of justified prose text, presents specific challenges to the scribes.

The tiny italic and formal script used for marginal notes is also very technically demanding, especially since these notes have to be readable even in the reduced size of the reproduction books. The notes are generally done by the scribe who wrote the majority of the text on each page.

Something that seems as simple as the chapter numbers is also a challenge for the Wales team. One difficulty is laying down a block of color. The paints and ink have to be fairly dry, because if they are too wet on the page the vellum may pucker at that spot. Also, what colors should they be? For the 219 colored boxes in this volume Donald Jackson, Sally Mae Joseph, and Brian Simpson made a sort of game of it. They took turns choosing colors from a selection pinned on a board and assigned them to a number. This way the colors would be somewhat randomly chosen, but also complement the other colors on the pages where they appeared.

Another quirk of the page numbers is the sizing. Despite computerized layouts of each page, they realized there was not enough space for large chapter numbers on each page.

Calligraphy

You'll notice there are two sizes of chapter headings. For example, look at Isaiah 20–23. The chapter numbers are significantly smaller than those on the following page (chs. 24–26).

THE ART OF THE SAINT JOHN'S BIBLE

What pieces of Ezekiel's vision can you identify in the illumination?

No matter how you view it, Ezekiel was an eccentric character. He acted out versions of the prophecy he was given for the people. He ate dung, lay on one side and then the other for years, and did not mourn for his wife when she died—all at God's direction. Readers wonder if Ezekiel's wild use of metaphors and images came from his own visionary character or from the disorientation he felt as an Israelite in exile.

Vision at the Chebar

EZEKIEL 1:1–3:27
As I was among the exiles by the river Chebar, the heavens were opened, and I saw visions of God. (1:1)

VISION AT THE CHEBAR

For the illumination of Ezekiel's first vision, Donald Jackson returned to the British Museum and to artifacts from the world of the Babylonian exile. His thinking about these visions was that they were probably made up of the kind of images the prophets and other exiles regularly saw in the temples and courts of the Babylonian Empire. He wanted to find images of figures and architectural details that might have fed the fearsome visions of the exiles. When Spanish conquistadors arrived in Latin America they often sent back outlandish, "visionary" accounts of what they saw. What we would take for granted now as merely exotic birds and wildlife were so strange to their European eyes that they could not make sense of what they saw.

In Ezekiel's description of the vision, he repeatedly says he saw "something like . . ." Built into his account is the fact that words can only approximate what he saw. When he describes the throne and rainbow of God's presence, he says "This was the appearance of the likeness of the glory of the LORD" (Ezek 1:28b). It is the glory of God seen through the lens of "likeness" and "appearance," never directly.

The elements of the vision are incorporated into the illumination, but there is no attempt to render a picture of what Ezekiel says he saw. In some ways the vision of four beasts with four heads, wings all around, and wheeled feet moving in any and all directions is too absurd to be drawn realistically. Again, Donald Jackson was struck by the description of noise in the passage: "I heard the sound of their wings like the sound of mighty waters, like the thunder of the Almighty, a sound of tumult like the sound of an army" (1:24). Even this short piece of a verse is packed with three similes: roaring water, thunder, and an army. The effect Donald Jackson wanted to convey was of the sound of the overwhelmingly strange and somewhat frightening vision that surrounded the exiles' camp.

There are three main elements in this illumination: the messengers, the wheels, and God's throne. The first are God's messengers. According to Donald Jackson there are enough pieces here—heads, legs, bodies—to make four complete creatures. The four heads for each have become important symbols in the Christian tradition. The human, lion, ox, and eagle are often used to represent the four evangelists: Matthew the human, Mark the lion, Luke the ox, and John the eagle.

The gloomy, spooky heads with yellow eyes usually strike people first. These figures are based on a low relief portrait on a ceramic lid of a casket made, it is said, under Greek influence. These burial masks certainly have an otherworldly feel. The eagle, ox, and lion heads likewise come from images out of that period and region.

At the top left is the image of the figure on the throne, with fragments of sapphires and rainbows. This passage is the source of the image of the rainbow for God's glory, and the rainbow continues at the bottom of the image and reappears on the next page where Ezekiel sits eating the scroll. On both sides of the scroll (both in the illumination and in this marginal piece) are printed the words "lamentation," "mourning," and "woe" (see Ezek 2:10). Still, when Ezekiel eats the scroll he says: "in my mouth it was as sweet as honey" (3:3).

The wheeled chariot throne is one of the famous images from Ezekiel. He describes the wheels as a wheel within a wheel. These wheels were based on Assyrian relief carvings. You will notice that the sides of the wheels actually have eyes, as described in the vision. However, Donald Jackson said a scholar at one of the exhibitions told him something interesting about those eyes. The scholar claimed that "eyes" was a mistranslation of a word that would otherwise mean bronze studs. The studs prevented wear to the rims, like tires. Going back to the source image, Donald saw that in fact the chariot wheel from the period did seem to have metal studs along the rim. Although he kept the more traditional image from the vision of wheels with eyes, it is certain that the actual wheels would have made quite a clatter as they passed through the streets, one source of the noise that probably frightened the exiles.

◀ *How does this image compare to Isaiah's call? How to Jeremiah's?*

VISION AT THE CHEBAR

Valley of Dry Bones

EZEKIEL 37:1-14

Prophesy to these bones, and say to them: O dry bones, hear the word of the LORD. (37:4)

What unusual images do you see in this valley? In what way are they comparable to "dry bones"?

This two-page illumination again draws on the contrasts between destruction and promise in Old Testament prophetic visions. In this case it is an image of the promise of new life to be breathed into the dry bones of a destroyed society. In Ezekiel 37, God takes Ezekiel to stand in a valley of bones and tells him, "these bones are the whole house of Israel" (37:11). The vision is of a dead people, a wasteland filled with the bones of the victims of many invasions. The people are not just physically dead; the entire society is spiritually dead and "dry," having turned from God. The montage along the bottom of the page points to the destruction of war, a contemporary valley of bones more like a trash heap, the detritus of a spiritually dead society.

Donald Jackson began this illumination with an internet search, a far cry from his research among the British Museum's antiquities. With the help of Sarah Harris he gathered a set of horrific documentary photos chronicling the human suffering of the recent past. The skulls are based on photos taken of genocide and war in Armenia, Rwanda, Iraq, and Bosnia. The piles of broken glass suggest the broken windows caused by car bombs, suicide bombers, and terrorist attacks, as well as the empty shells of vandalized and abandoned buildings. At the center is a pile of eyeglasses, a well-known image from the Holocaust. This image is mixed with a heap of bones, skulls, broken glass, and trashed automobiles. For Donald Jackson the waste of ecological disaster is part of the larger image of the valley filled with bones. The automobile hulls (there are three) are one sign of the spiritual death of society.

Among the wreckage, however, there is a glimmer of hope. The lightly colored spot on the right side is an oil slick. Just as an oily puddle will appear to have a rainbow on its surface, so also in the midst of this valley of dry bones there is hope and God's presence. The gold squares that have been used throughout the volumes of *The Saint John's*

Bible to indicate the presence of the divine are also here even in the darkest spaces of the image. Indeed, the words along the bottom of the page speak of promise, not judgment: "I will put my spirit within you and you shall live."

Dramatically different from the heaps of death and destruction is the rainbow across the top of the page. These overlapping circles of rainbow seem torn and pasted, again as in a collage. The image foreshadows what is to come a few pages later, in Ezekiel's vision of the temple.

Finally, the image is punctuated by seven menorahs, a link to creation and covenant. The menorah has been an ongoing sign of the covenant between God and the people in *The Saint John's Bible* since Genesis. We have seen it with *Abraham and Sarah* (Gen 15 and 17) and again in the *Genealogy of Christ* (Matt 1). Here the seven gold and black bars are intersected by arcs that end in points of light. Seven menorahs with seven points of light rise out of and transcend the wreckage and wrongdoings of humankind, a sign of the renewal of both creation and the covenant described at the end of Ezekiel 37. The illumination *Creation* included a 7 x 7 grid of gold squares, and these squares are turned to make up the forty-nine points of light here. Seven is a symbolic number, meaning completion or totality. There is a contrast between what God has envisioned for Creation and what humans have made of it. Despite the darkness, it is always God's faithfulness and promise that predominate.

devour people and no longer bereave your nation of children, says the Lord GOD; and no longer will I let you hear the insults of the nations, no longer shall you bear the disgrace of the peoples; and no longer shall you cause your nation to stumble, says the Lord GOD. ¶ The word of the LORD came to me: Mortal, when the house of Israel lived on their own soil, they defiled it with their ways and their deeds; their conduct in my sight was like the uncleanness of a woman in her menstrual period. So I poured out my wrath upon them for the blood that they had shed upon the land, and for the idols with which they had defiled it; I scattered them among the nations, and they were dispersed through the countries; in accordance with their conduct & their deeds I judged them. But when they came to the nations, wherever they came, they profaned my holy name, in that it was said of them, "These are the people of the LORD, and yet they had to go out of his land." But I had concern for my holy name, which the house of Israel had profaned among the nations to which they came. ¶ Therefore say to the house of Israel, Thus says the Lord GOD: It is not for your sake, O house of Israel, that I am about to act, but for the sake of my holy name, which you have profaned among the nations to which you came. I will sanctify my great name, which has been profaned among the nations, and which you have profaned among them; and the nations shall know that I am the LORD, says the Lord GOD, when through you I display my holiness before their eyes. I will take you from the nations, and gather you from all the countries, and bring you into your own land. I will sprinkle clean water upon you, and you shall be clean from all your uncleannesses, and from all your idols I will cleanse you. A new heart I will give you, and a new spirit I will put within you; and I will remove

from your body the heart of stone and give you a heart of flesh. I will put my spirit within you, and make you follow my statutes and be careful to observe my ordinances. Then you shall live in the land that I gave to your ancestors; and you shall be my people, and I will be your God. I will save you from all your uncleannesses, and I will summon the grain and make it abundant and lay no famine upon you. I will make the fruit of the tree and the produce of the field abundant, so that you may never again suffer the disgrace of famine among the nations. Then you shall remember your evil ways, and your dealings that were not good; and you shall loathe yourselves for your iniquities and your abominable deeds. It is not for your sake that I will act, says the Lord GOD; let that be known to you. Be ashamed & dismayed for your ways, O house of Israel. ¶ Thus says the Lord GOD: On the day that I cleanse you from all your iniquities, I will cause the towns to be inhabited, and the waste places shall be rebuilt. The land that was desolate shall be tilled, instead of being the desolation that it was in the sight of all who passed by. And they will say, "This land that was desolate has become like the garden of Eden; and the waste and desolate and ruined towns are now inhabited and fortified." Then the nations that are left all around you shall know that I, the LORD, have rebuilt the ruined places, and replanted that which was desolate; I, the LORD, have spoken, and I will do it. ¶ Thus says the Lord GOD: I will also let the house of Israel ask me to do this for them: to increase their population like a flock. Like the flock for sacrifices, like the flock at Jerusalem during her appointed festivals, so shall the ruined towns be filled with flocks of people. Then they shall know that I am the LORD.

I WILL PUT MY SPIRIT

VALLEY OF DRY BONES

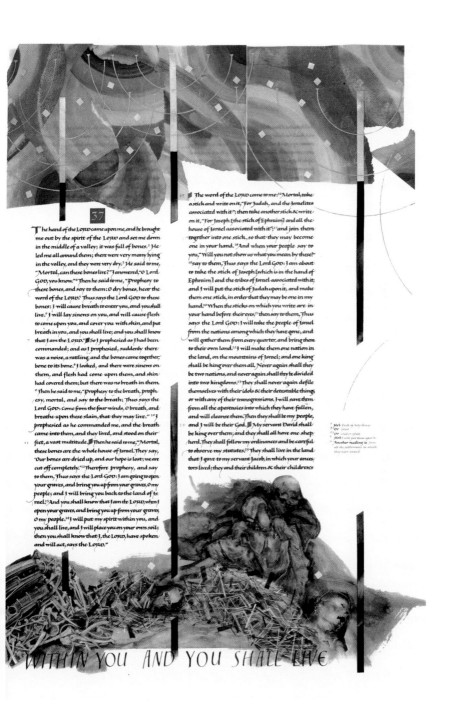

The hand of the LORD came upon me, and he brought me out by the spirit of the LORD and set me down in the middle of a valley; it was full of bones. ² He led me all around them; there were very many lying in the valley, and they were very dry. ³ He said to me, "Mortal, can these bones live?" I answered, "O Lord GOD, you know." ⁴ Then he said to me, "Prophesy to these bones, and say to them: O dry bones, hear the word of the LORD. ⁵ Thus says the Lord GOD to these bones: I will cause breath to enter you, and you shall live. ⁶ I will lay sinews on you, and will cause flesh to come upon you, and cover you with skin, and put breath in you, and you shall live; and you shall know that I am the LORD." ⁷ So I prophesied as I had been commanded; and as I prophesied, suddenly there was a noise, a rattling, and the bones came together, bone to its bone. ⁸ I looked, and there were sinews on them, and flesh had come upon them, and skin had covered them; but there was no breath in them. ⁹ Then he said to me, "Prophesy to the breath, prophesy, mortal, and say to the breath: Thus says the Lord GOD: Come from the four winds, O breath, and breathe upon these slain, that they may live." ¹⁰ I prophesied as he commanded me, and the breath came into them, and they lived, and stood on their feet, a vast multitude. ¹¹ Then he said to me, "Mortal, these bones are the whole house of Israel. They say, 'Our bones are dried up, and our hope is lost; we are cut off completely.' ¹² Therefore prophesy, and say to them, Thus says the Lord GOD: I am going to open your graves, and bring you up from your graves, O my people; and I will bring you back to the land of Israel. ¹³ And you shall know that I am the LORD, when I open your graves, and bring you up from your graves, O my people. ¹⁴ I will put my spirit within you, and you shall live, and I will place you on your own soil; then you shall know that I, the LORD, have spoken and will act, says the LORD."

¹⁵ The word of the LORD came to me: ¹⁶ Mortal, take a stick and write on it, "For Judah, and the Israelites associated with it"; then take another stick & write on it, "For Joseph [the stick of Ephraim] and all the house of Israel associated with it"; ¹⁷ and join them together into one stick, so that they may become one in your hand. ¹⁸ And when your people say to you, "Will you not show us what you mean by these?" ¹⁹ say to them, Thus says the Lord GOD: I am about to take the stick of Joseph [which is in the hand of Ephraim] and the tribes of Israel associated with it; and I will put the stick of Judah upon it, and make them one stick, in order that they may be one in my hand. ²⁰ When the sticks on which you write are in your hand before their eyes, ²¹ then say to them, Thus says the Lord GOD: I will take the people of Israel from the nations among which they have gone, and will gather them from every quarter, and bring them to their own land. ²² I will make them one nation in the land, on the mountains of Israel; and one king shall be king over them all. Never again shall they be two nations, and never again shall they be divided into two kingdoms. ²³ They shall never again defile themselves with their idols & their detestable things or with any of their transgressions. I will save them from all the apostasies into which they have fallen, and will cleanse them. Then they shall be my people, and I will be their God. ²⁴ My servant David shall be king over them; and they shall all have one shepherd. They shall follow my ordinances and be careful to observe my statutes. ²⁵ They shall live in the land that I gave to my servant Jacob, in which your ancestors lived; they and their children & their children's

Heb flesh of help things
Or wind
Heb I will not show upon it
Another reading is from all the settlements in which they have sinned

WITHIN YOU AND YOU SHALL LIVE

Vision of the New Temple

EZEKIEL 40:1–48:35

Mortal, this is the place of my throne and the place for the soles of my feet, where I will reside among the people of Israel forever. (Ezek 43:7)

What does this architectural map of the temple remind you of?

The destruction of the temple in Jerusalem is the sign of absolute destruction for the people of Israel in exile. In Ezekiel 10 and 11 the prophet has a vision of God leaving the temple on his throne-chariot. This vision assigns blame for their downfall to the people of Israel, whose disobedience and worship of idols in effect drive God from their midst. The vision of God's return to the temple is a vision of renewal and restored covenant.

The book of Ezekiel spends a total of eight full chapters describing this vision! In it the Lord lays out a blueprint for rebuilding the temple, although it is not a blueprint any architect would want to follow. Still, people have tried, and the basis for this illumination is a seventeenth-century engraving for a Dutch reconstruction (on a smaller scale) of Solomon's temple. The engraving has been digitally manipulated to give the effect of a vision, and turned into more of a labyrinth or maze than a blueprint. A gold ribbon, used at the beginning and end of this volume with the wing motif, metaphorically traces Ezekiel's path through the labyrinth. In this way the vision again speaks to the theme of transformation, this time in terms of a journey. The prophet takes a winding path through the areas of the new temple, with plenty of backtracking and long loops, much like the circuitous path of Israel back to God. As Donald Jackson has said about this image, it is better to get lost in the labyrinth seeking God's holy of holies if it means truly finding oneself.

The vision is also eschatological, a description of the eternal temple of God. The journey is not logical or straightforward, but belongs to the world of the vision. After being taken to various areas by "a man who shone like bronze" (40:3), measuring various areas of the courts, Ezekiel says, "The spirit lifted me up and brought me into the inner court" (43:5). At the top of a mountain at the center of the temple Ezekiel is shown God's ultimate plan. This temple is not about the present, but is the eternal home of God where all people will come to worship. Ezekiel is not the only prophet to have a more apocalyptic vision of the end of time. The prophet Daniel speaks particularly of the kingdom of God as a place that will endure forever. Further, in the New Testament Jesus compares himself to the temple at Jerusalem, saying he will pull down the temple and rebuild it in three days, referring to his death and resurrection.

In a way the vision of the temple is a creation story, and the garden at the East gate is a restoration of the Garden of

VISION OF THE NEW TEMPLE

ראובן · Reuben

יהודה · Judah

לוי · Levi

יוסף · Joseph

בנימין · Benjamin

דן · Dan

שמעון · Simeon

יששכר · Issachar

זבולון · Zebulun

גד · Gad

אשר · Asher

בפתלי · Naphtali

TRIBES OF ISRAEL

Eden. Outside the East gate are images described in the vision. The palm trees are based on Assyrian engravings. The egret images come from Egyptian wall paintings of the eighteenth-century dynasty at Karnack. The fish stamps appear again, as in the illumination *Loaves and Fishes* in the book of Mark. The new creation, like the old creation, will populate the earth, sea, and air, and the focus is on fruitfulness and fertility.

The gold block we have come to associate with God's throne is at the base of the temple gate through which God enters in the vision. The glory of the Lord, in the form of a rainbow, does indeed fill every space in the temple. The technique makes it look as if the paint is absorbed into the vellum like stain, as though it saturates the entire space with color. The effect is that the illumination is enhanced and, combined with the manipulated grid, takes the viewer to the mesmerizing space of the vision, out of the mundane world of "cubits."

On the facing page the twelve tribes of Israel are placed beneath the letter standing for their gate, as is prescribed in the biblical text. It is significant that all twelve tribes are listed, a sign of further restoration. At the time of the destruction of the first temple of Jerusalem the only tribes still in the Promised Land were Benjamin and Judah. The ten tribes to the north, named after the other heirs of Jacob, are sometimes referred to as the "lost tribes" of Israel. Little record of them exists following the Assyrian invasion in the eighth century B.C.E. Here, however, they are reunited as guards of the four gates, three tribes on each side, another sign of the apocalyptic nature of the vision.

A few pages later is a delicate piece of marginalia. The papaya tree makes the connection with the medicinal and food trees mentioned in the Vision of the Temple. Young trees like this are at the heart of reforestation projects throughout the world.

Although not a special text treatment, the litany sung by Shadrach, Meshach, and Abednego while in the fiery furnace makes for an impressive piece of calligraphy that again demonstrates what it means that this Bible is written by hand. Here Sally Mae Joseph wrote "Bless the Lord" and the refrain "sing praise to him and highly exalt him forever" forty-three times. You can see the slight variation in the capital *B* and the tail of the *f* of "forever." Like a work of fine craftsmanship, *The Saint John's Bible* could be stamped: "Handmade: no two alike" or "variations in the text are due to the nature of the process" as is found on some hand-woven goods to reflect natural variation in wool. Here the variation draws attention to the consistency and craft, and adds beauty to the poem. An artist has sat at the table before a piece of vellum, with quill and ink, and written these lines. This song is also marked at the beginning with a cross in the margin, and the note "RSB." That means this verse is referenced in the Rule of Benedict. Also part of the Liturgy of the Hours, this litany is one of the texts for Sunday Morning Prayer.

Bless the Lord

DANIEL 3:52-90

DANIEL

⁵⁵ Blessed are you on the throne of your kingdom,
  and to be extolled and highly exalted forever.
⁵⁶ Blessed are you in the firmament of heaven,
  and to be sung and glorified forever.

⁵⁷ "Bless the Lord, all you works of the Lord;
  sing praise to him and highly exalt him forever.
⁵⁸ Bless the Lord you heavens;
  sing praise to him and highly exalt him forever.
⁵⁹ Bless the Lord, you angels of the Lord;
  sing praise to him and highly exalt him forever.
⁶⁰ Bless the Lord, all you waters above the heavens;
  sing praise to him and highly exalt him forever.
⁶¹ Bless the Lord, all you powers of the Lord;
  sing praise to him and highly exalt him forever.
⁶² Bless the Lord, sun and moon;
  sing praise to him and highly exalt him forever.
⁶³ Bless the Lord, stars of heaven;
  sing praise to him and highly exalt him forever.

⁶⁴ "Bless the Lord, all rain and dew;
  sing praise to him and highly exalt him forever.
⁶⁵ Bless the Lord, all you winds;
  sing praise to him and highly exalt him forever.
⁶⁶ Bless the Lord, fire and heat;
  sing praise to him and highly exalt him forever.
⁶⁷ Bless the Lord, winter cold and summer heat;
  sing praise to him and highly exalt him forever.
⁶⁸ Bless the Lord, dews and falling snow;
  sing praise to him and highly exalt him forever.
⁶⁹ Bless the Lord, ice and cold;
  sing praise to him and highly exalt him forever.
⁷⁰ Bless the Lord, frosts and snows;
  sing praise to him and highly exalt him forever.
⁷¹ Bless the Lord, nights and days;
  sing praise to him and highly exalt him forever.
⁷² Bless the Lord, light and darkness;
  sing praise to him and highly exalt him forever.
⁷³ Bless the Lord, lightnings and clouds;
  sing praise to him and highly exalt him forever.

⁷⁴ "Let the earth bless the Lord;
  let it sing praise to him & highly exalt him forever.
⁷⁵ Bless the Lord, mountains and hills;
  sing praise to him and highly exalt him forever.
⁷⁶ Bless the Lord, all that grows in the ground;
  sing praise to him and highly exalt him forever.
⁷⁷ Bless the Lord, you springs;
  sing praise to him and highly exalt him forever.
⁷⁸ Bless the Lord, seas and rivers;
  sing praise to him and highly exalt him forever.
⁷⁹ Bless the Lord, you whales and all that
  swim in the waters;
  sing praise to him and highly exalt him forever.

ʲ Gk: hand
ᵏ Aram a sense of the gods
ˡ Meaning of Aram
  word uncertain

DANIEL 3:52-90

Vision of the Son of Man

DANIEL 7:1-28
I, Daniel, saw in my vision by night . . . (7:2)

What elements of destruction and elements of hope do you see here?

This illumination by Donald Jackson includes a contribution by Aidan Hart, an icon painter who has done many of the faces in the volumes. In this vision Donald Jackson suggested that he render the face of Christ in monochromatic blue, a challenge for someone used to dealing in traditional flesh tones. The face here can be compared with the image of Christ in the *Sower and the Seed* (Mark 4:3-9).

Daniel's vision was a source for the author of the book of Revelation and is classified more as apocalyptic literature

VISION OF THE SON OF MAN

THE ART OF THE SAINT JOHN'S BIBLE

than as prophecy. It seems to describe the final working out of God's plan, although it also addresses the immediate situation of the people. Apocalyptic literature can be found in many cultures and even in more recent times, for example in Native American or postcolonial African literature. It tends to be written in times of extreme persecution, when the situation looks hopeless and only supernatural intervention seems able to turn things around. The dream of the four beasts parallels the rule of the empires of Babylon, Medea, Persia, and finally Greece. After the Babylonian exile and return to Jerusalem under the Persians, Israel remained an occupied land. The Greeks in particular tried to assimilate Israel to its culture and religious practices. It is easy to see why the author of Revelation, living in a time of extreme persecution under the Romans, would turn to the book of Daniel for inspiration.

The two sides of this diptych represent the two sides of the vision. On the left is the great beast, with its ten horns and tusks and fiery eyes. You can also see the small horn among the ten that has an eye and "a mouth speaking arrogantly." The background is based on enlarged images of streptococcus bacteria, a contemporary form of a devouring beast. This kingdom is described in the explanation of the vision as "a fourth kingdom on earth that shall . . . devour the whole earth, and trample it down, and break it to pieces" (Dan 7:23). This was understood as describing the Greek Empire, and the arrogant, persecuting little horn the Emperor Antiochus Epiphanes, who gained power by uprooting others. That Daniel should have this vision fits the narrative. His fame within the Babylonian Empire became well-known at King Belshazzar's feast (Dan 5:1-30), where Daniel interprets the vision of the handwriting on the wall.

More interesting in this vision is the dual image of God, the deliverer. On the left side we see an image of the Ancient One. As in earlier visions of the prophets, the figure is pictured on a throne, this time with clothing "white as snow" (7:9). The throne is surrounded by rainbow blocks, the motif for the glory of God we also saw in Isaiah and Ezekiel. Daniel describes wheels of fire, and the wheel stamps from Ezekiel's *Vision at the Chebar* are here on a field of red. One of the wheels is grinding over the beast with four leopard heads sketched in black. Looking closely, you can see the image of a multitude, like a crowd of "thousand thousands" at the foot of the throne. The left panel, then, shows the overthrow of the great beast by the Ancient One, the God of Israel, that has been depicted throughout the books of the prophets.

This part of the image is linked to the right-hand side by a grid reminiscent of the temple path in Ezekiel. Icons also use these geometric frames to highlight a divine image. Here two strains of the prophecies—the ongoing reign of God and the messianic visions—come together. Daniel not only sees the Ancient One, but also the Son of Man. Before we look at this more closely, a note needs to be made on the translation. The NRSV reads, "I saw one coming like a human being," with a note in the margin explaining that an alternative translation of the term used here is "son of man." The NRSV has chosen "human being" because the translators aim to choose more gender-inclusive language when possible. However, in doing so it loses the connection to Jesus calling himself the Son of Man in the gospels. The term "son of man" is Aramaic for "someone" or "somebody." In the gospels it takes on the role of a proper title, "Son of Man," and it is this that the early writers use as a reference to Christ. *The Saint John's Bible* maintains that connection by using an icon of Christ as the Son of Man. Daniel's vision describes the relationship between the Father and the Son.

Unlike Isaiah's messianic visions that stressed the suffering servant or a child, here the messiah comes as the triumphant one sent from the skies to have "everlasting dominion" and establish a kingdom that will never pass away. The figure here is a depiction of the prophecy, as is the image on the left. The Son of Man is seen coming "with the clouds of heaven." Above his head are the gold boxes that signal the presence of divinity. His feet are planted on the earth, and beneath his feet is a stamp like a rich carpet. This stamp was used to adorn the robes of the risen Christ when he appears to Mary Magdalene in John 20.

THE ART OF THE SAINT JOHN'S BIBLE

What does this passage tell us about God's mercy and judgment?

In another section of this guide we discuss the work of Suzanne Moore and her illumination *Praise of Wisdom* in Sirach. In addition to illuminations, she has also done two text treatments for earlier volumes, *Choose Life* (Deut 30:19-20) and *The Lord Bless You* (Num 6:24).

Moore has commented that the passages she has dealt with in the project have all been about choice, the alternatives of light and dark, obedience and disobedience. They all demonstrate human responsibility for our own destiny as we respond to God's promises. The connection between Deuteronomy 30 and Amos 4 seems very direct. Deuteronomy 30 begins with a prediction of the exile, naming it as one of the curses that will come upon Israel as a consequence of disobedience. The opening verses read:

> When all these things have happened to you, the blessings and the curses that I have set before you, if you call them to mind among all the nations where the LORD your God has driven you, and *return to the LORD your God,* and you and your children obey him with all your heart and with all your soul, just as I am commanding you today, then the LORD your God will restore your fortunes and have compassion on you, gathering

Demands of Social Justice

AMOS 4
The locust devoured your fig trees and your olive trees; yet you did not return to me, says the Lord. (4:9b)

you again from all the peoples among whom the LORD your God has scattered you." (vv. 1-3)

Deuteronomy 30 ends with the passage treated by Suzanne Moore:

> I call heaven and earth to witness against you today that I have set before you life and death, blessings and curses. Choose life so that you and your descendants may live, loving the LORD your God, obeying him, and holding fast to him; for that means life to you and length of days, so that you may live in the land that the LORD swore to give to your ancestors, to Abraham, to Isaac, and to Jacob.

The people have a choice, to follow the commandments and thus "choose life," or to disrupt God's order and turn from God's blessings. In this passage from Amos, God's lament is that, despite all that God has done to try to draw Israel back, they do not return. So the poetry of verses 6-11 lists God's attempts to get Israel's attention: lack of bread; drought; blight, mildew, and locusts; pestilence, war, and defeat. The refrain rings out poignantly, as we feel God's sadness: *"yet you did not return to me."* It is these words that Moore has taken for her illumination. She sees them, fragmented and repeated, as a sign of the fragmentation of Creation itself. For the primary text in gold boxes she used the same script as for *Choose Life*, heightening the connection between the two passages.

The illumination is broken into seven pieces, but the pieces are not even and ordered like the days of *Creation*. Inside them, the black, blue, and green panels representing sky, sea, and earth are also not fruitful and ordered, but chaotic. This is a reminder that God did not just try to turn the people's hearts with plagues and punishments, but first tried to draw them close with all the beauty, order, and fruitfulness of the Garden. It is the people's choice not to follow God that has made creation this way.

The book of Amos is known for its vision of social justice. The fractured words also refer to the ways injustice and inequality fracture society. At the heart of this prophecy, however, is a reminder of the law and the covenant. God is a God of compassion, not violence and punishment. The people have a choice, and yet they turn from God and do not put in place the society that welcomes God and in which God can live.

THE ART OF THE SAINT JOHN'S BIBLE

Another motto close to the hearts of Benedictines comes from Micah 6:8. Sally Mae Joseph's text treatment is again of a piece with the others in the volume, and again points to God's goodness and desire to see humans act with love. The people ask the question: "With what shall I come before the LORD?" Wanting to make amends for their transgressions and regain God's favor, they wonder what kind and number of sacrifices God will require. The passage here is the answer, and it highlights three Benedictine values: justice, hospitality, and humility. God does not want sacrifices but right behavior, and longs for a people who "do justice," "love kindness," and "walk humbly" with God.

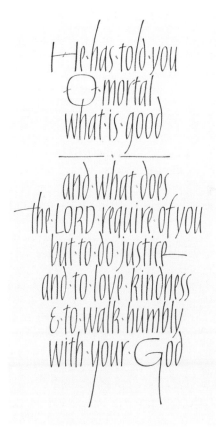

MICAH 6:8

Rejoice!

ZECHARIAH 9:9-17; 10:1-5
*Lo, your king comes to you;
triumphant and victorious is
he, humble and riding on a
donkey, on a colt, the foal of
a donkey. (9:9b)*

*Are the words and images in this illumination
complementary or in tension?*

This final messianic vision is by Hazel Dolby and includes
text from Zechariah 9:9: "Lo, your king comes to you; triumphant and victorious is he." However, the tone of the
image is not what we might expect for an illumination titled
"Rejoice!" For that mood we would do better to return to
Messianic Predictions in Isaiah. This image draws on the link
made between this passage in Zechariah and the Triumphant Entry celebrated on Palm Sunday. Jesus arrives in
Jerusalem on a donkey, greeted by people singing Hosanna
and calling him the messiah, the Son of David, laying down
palms in his path (Matt 21:1-10). He does not come to rule,
however, but to prepare for his crucifixion.

זכריה

⁹ Rejoice greatly, O daughter Zion!
    Shout aloud, O daughter Jerusalem!
Lo, your king comes to you;
    triumphant and victorious is he,
    humble and riding on a donkey,
    on a colt, the foal of a donkey.

and be full like a bowl,
    drenched like the corners of the altar.

¹⁶ On that day the LORD their God will save them
    for they are the flock of his people;
    for like the jewels of a crown
        they shall shine on his land.
¹⁷ For what goodness and beauty are his!
    Grain shall make the young men flourish,
    and new wine the young women.

LO, YOUR KING COMES TO YOU

TRIUMPHANT AND VICTORIOUS IS HE

¹⁰ He will cut off the chariot from Ephraim
    and the war-horse from Jerusalem;
    and the battle bow shall be cut off,
    and he shall command peace to the nations;
    his dominion shall be from sea to sea,
    and from the River to the ends of the earth.

¹¹ As for you also, because of the blood of my
        covenant with you,
    I will set your prisoners free from
        the waterless pit.

10

Ask rain from the LORD
    in the season of the spring rain,
from the LORD who makes the storm clouds,
    who gives showers of rain to you,
    the vegetation in the field to everyone.
² For the teraphim utter nonsense,
    and the diviners see lies;

REJOICE!

THE ART OF THE SAINT JOHN'S BIBLE

"The king" here arrives on a donkey, with head bowed. The donkey is a colt, and the man's feet hang almost to the ground. Even the donkey looks sad! The palm trees remind us of Palm Sunday but also of Ezekiel's vision of the temple with its palm trees in the garden outside the gate. In the upper left hand corner of the image is the shadow of a city. This is another indication that the vision has an eschatological dimension. The kingdom is not of this world, not even of Jesus' time, but will be reached eventually. Victory, we are being told here, is not found in the portrait of a proud, conquering hero, but in our Suffering Servant.

This is the last illumination in *Prophets*, aside from the closing motif of the winged seraphs and temple grid. It is quiet, and filled with paradox, like the beginning of the Christian Holy Week. Jesus rides the donkey to Jerusalem, aware of what will happen there. What will happen is necessary for the ultimate glory of Easter and salvation and the final glorious vision of God's kingdom. It is proper that the book ends with a vision of a journey. All of these prophets have taken their own journeys, responded to the call, and acted their part in salvation history.

❧ *What is God's call to us? How will we respond?*

Index of Visual Elements

MARGINALIA:

Isaiah 30	*Scarab*	Chris Tomlin
Jeremiah 17	*Two Field Crickets*	Chris Tomlin
Jeremiah 35	*Cicada*	Chris Tomlin
Ezekiel 22	*Black Fly*	Chris Tomlin
Ezekiel 47:12	*Papaya Tree*	Sally Mae Joseph
Wisdom 7	*Correction Bee*	Chris Tomlin and Sarah Harris

BLACK FLY

PAPAYA TREE

THE ART OF THE SAINT JOHN'S BIBLE

Isaiah 1:16-17   Wash yourselves; make yourselves clean;
                      remove the evil of your doings
                      from before my eyes;
                  cease to do evil,
                      learn to do good;
                  seek justice,
                      rescue the oppressed,
                  defend the orphan,
                      plead for the widow.
                                        Sally Mae Joseph

Isaiah 2:4   He shall judge between the nations,
                      and shall arbitrate for many peoples;
                  they shall beat their swords into plowshares,
                      and their spears into pruning hooks;
                  nation shall not lift up sword against nation,
                      neither shall they learn war any more.
                                        Sally Mae Joseph

Isaiah 40:1-5   Comfort, O comfort, my people,
                      says your GOD.
                  Speak tenderly to Jerusalem,
                      and cry to her
                  that she has served her term,
                      that her penalty is paid,
                  that she has received from the LORD's hand
                      double for all her sins.

                  A voice cries out:
                      "In the wilderness prepare the way of the LORD,
                      make straight in the desert a highway for our God.
                  Every valley shall be lifted up,
                      and every mountain and hill made low;
                  the uneven ground shall become level,
                      and the rough places a plain.
                  Then the glory of the LORD shall be revealed,
                      and all people shall see it together,
                      for the mouth of the LORD has spoken."
                                        Sally Mae Joseph

Isaiah 49:1-4   Listen to me, O coastlands,
                      pay attention, you peoples from far away!
                  The LORD called me before I was born,
                      while I was in my mother's womb he named me.
                  He made my mouth like a sharp sword,

in the shadow of his hand he hid me;
he made me a polished arrow;
in his quiver he hid me away.
And he said to me, "You are my servant,
Israel, in whom I will be glorified."
But I said, "I have labored in vain,
I have spent my strength for nothing and vanity;
yet surely my cause is with the LORD,
and my reward with my God."

Sally Mae Joseph

Isaiah 60:1-3   Arise, shine; for your light has come,
and the glory of the LORD has risen upon you.
For darkness shall cover the earth,
and thick darkness the peoples;
but the LORD will arise upon you,
and his glory will appear over you.
Nations shall come to your light,
and kings to the brightness of your dawn.

Sally Mae Joseph

Isaiah 66:12-13   For thus says the LORD:
I will extend prosperity to her like a river,
and the wealth of the nations like an overflowing stream;
and you shall nurse and be carried on her arm,
and dandled on her knees.
As a mother comforts her child,
so I will comfort you;
you shall be comforted in Jerusalem.

Thomas Ingmire

Jeremiah 1:4-10   Now the word of the LORD came to me saying,
"Before I formed you in the womb I knew you,
and before you were born I consecrated you;
I appointed you a prophet to the nations."
Then I said, "Ah, Lord GOD! Truly I do not know how to speak,
for I am only a boy." But the LORD said to me,
"Do not say, 'I am only a boy';
for you shall go to all to whom I send you,
and you shall speak whatever I command you,
for I am with you to deliver you,
says the LORD."
Then the LORD put out his hand and touched my mouth; and the
LORD said to me,

THE ART OF THE SAINT JOHN'S BIBLE

"Now I have put my words in your mouth.
See, today I appoint you over nations and over kingdoms,
to pluck up and to pull down,
to destroy and to overthrow,
to build and to plant."

Sally Mae Joseph

Micah 6:8
He has told you, O mortal, what is good;
and what does the LORD require of you
but to do justice, and to love kindness,
and to walk humbly with your God.

Sally Mae Joseph

Wisdom 6:12
Wisdom is radiant and unfading,
and she is easily discerned by
those who love her,
and is found by those who seek her.

(This text receives two special treatments,
one found at Job 15 by *Angela Swan* and the
other alongside the actual verse as part of a
longer treatment by *Sally Mae Joseph*.)

Job 19:25
For I know that my Redeemer lives,
and that at the last he will stand upon the earth.

Diane M. von Arx

Proverbs 1:7-8
The fear of the LORD is the beginning of knowledge;
fools despise wisdom and instruction.
Hear, my child, your father's instruction,
and do not reject your mother's teaching.

Thomas Ingmire

Ecclesiastes 11:1
Send out your bread upon the waters,
for after many days you will get it back.

Diane M. von Arx

ECCLESIASTES 11:1

INDEX

Wisdom 4:7-9

But the righteous, though they die early, will be at rest.
For old age is not honored for length of time,
or measured by number of years;
but understanding is gray hair for anyone,
and a blameless life is ripe old age.

Sally Mae Joseph

Wisdom 6:12-18

Wisdom is radiant and unfading,
and she is easily discerned by those who love her,
and is found by those who seek her.
She hastens to make herself known to those who desire her.
One who rises early to seek her will have no difficulty,
for she will be found sitting at the gate.
To fix one's thought on her is perfect understanding,
and one who is vigilant on her account will soon be free from care,
because she goes about seeking those worthy of her,
and she graciously appears to them in their paths,
and meets them in every thought.

The beginning of wisdom is the most sincere desire for instruction,
and concern for instruction is love of her,
and love of her is the keeping of her laws,
and giving heed to her laws is assurance of immortality,
and immortality brings one near to God;
so the desire for wisdom leads to a kingdom.

Sally Mae Joseph

Sirach 1:16

To fear the Lord is fullness of wisdom;
she inebriates mortals with her fruits;
she fills their whole house with desirable goods,
and their storehouses with her produce.

Brian Simpson

Sirach 6:14-22 Faithful friends are a sturdy shelter:
whoever finds one has found a treasure.
Faithful friends are beyond price;
no amount can balance their worth.
Faithful friends are life-saving medicine,
and those who fear the Lord will find them.
Those who fear the Lord direct their friendship aright,
for as they are, so are their neighbors also.

My child, from your youth choose discipline,
and when you have gray hair you will still find wisdom.
Come to her like one who plows and sows,

THE ART OF THE SAINT JOHN'S BIBLE

and wait for her good harvest.
For when you cultivate her you will toil but little,
and soon you will eat of her produce.
She seems very harsh to the undisciplined;
fools cannot remain with her.
She will be like a heavy stone to test them,
and they will not delay in casting her aside.
For wisdom is like her name;
she is not readily perceived by many.

Diane M. von Arx

Sirach 24:19

Come to me, you who desire me,
and eat your fill of my fruits,
for the memory of me is sweeter than honey,
and the possession of me sweeter than the honeycomb.

Sally Mae Joseph

(The treatment is found at Sirach 13 because
that page includes a full-scale illumination,
Praise of Wisdom)

Sirach 33:13

Like clay in the hand of the potter,
to be molded as he pleases,
so all are in the hand of their Maker,
to be given whatever he decides.

Donald Jackson

Wisdom 7:26

She is a reflection of eternal light,
a spotless mirror of the working of God,
and an image of his goodness.

Susie Leiper

(Found at Sirach 35 because Wisdom 7–8 includes another text treatment and the full-
scale illumination Wisdom Woman)

Sirach 39:13-15

Listen to me, my faithful children, and blossom
like a rose growing by a stream of water.
Send out fragrance like incense,
and put forth blossoms like a lily.
Scatter the fragrance, and sing a hymn of praise;
bless the Lord for all his works.
Ascribe majesty to his name

WISDOM 7:26

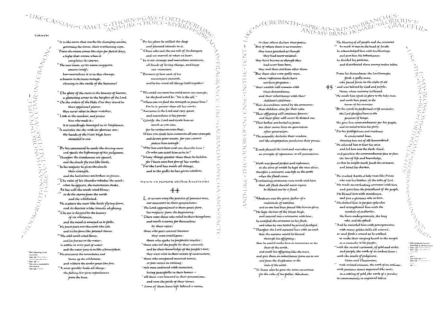

and give thanks to him with praise,
with songs on your lips, and with harps;
this is what you shall say in thanksgiving.

Diane M. von Arx

Sirach 24:12, 13, 15-17

I took root in an honored people . . .
I grew tall like a cedar in Lebanon . . .
Like cassia and camel's thorn, I gave forth perfume,
  and like choice myrrh I spread my fragrance,
like galbanum, onycha, and stacte,
  and like the odor of incense in the tent.
Like a terebinth I spread out my branches,
  and my branches are glorious and graceful.
Like the vine I bud forth delights,
  and my blossoms become glorious and abundant fruit.

Sue Hufton

(Found at Sirach 45 because of the full-scale
illumination Praise of Wisdom at Sirach 24)

THE ART OF THE SAINT JOHN'S BIBLE

ILLUMINATORS

Donald Jackson (Artistic Director and Illuminator — Monmouthshire, Wales)

One of the world's leading calligraphers, Donald Jackson is the artistic director and illuminator of *The Saint John's Bible*. From his scriptorium in Wales he oversees scribes, artists, and craftsmen who work with him on the handwriting and illumination of this seven-volume, 1,150-page book. His studio/workshop is the only calligraphy atelier in the United Kingdom where artist calligraphers are still regularly employed as assistants, maintaining the highest traditions of this ancient art in a modern context.

From an early age Jackson sought to combine the use of the ancient techniques of the calligrapher's art with the imagery and spontaneous letter forms of his own time. As a teenager his first ambition was to be "The Queen's Scribe" and a close second was to inscribe and illuminate the Bible. His talents were soon recognized and his ambitions fulfilled.

At the age of twenty, while still a student himself, Jackson was appointed a visiting lecturer (professor) at the Camberwell College of Art, London. Within six years he became the youngest artist calligrapher chosen to take part in the Victoria and Albert Museum's first International Calligraphy Show after the war and was appointed a scribe to the Crown Office at the House of Lords. As a scribe to Her Majesty Queen Elizabeth II he was responsible for the creation of official state documents. In conjunction with a wide range of other calligraphic projects he executed Historic Royal documents under The Great Seal and Royal Charters. In 1985 he was decorated by the Queen with the Medal of The Royal Victorian Order (MVO), which is awarded for personal services to the Sovereign.

Jackson is an elected Fellow and past Chairman of the prestigious Society of Scribes and Illuminators, and in 1997 was named Master of the six-hundred-year-old Guild of Scriveners of the city of London. His personally innovative work and inspirational teaching, together with books, a film series, and exhibitions in Europe, North America, Puerto Rico, Australia, and China have led to his being widely acknowledged as a seminal influence on the growth of Western calligraphy over the past twenty-five years. In 1980 he wrote *The Story of Writing,* which has since been published in many editions and seven languages. His thirty-year retrospective exhibition, *Painting With Words,* premiered at the Minneapolis Institute of Arts in Minneapolis, Minnesota in August 1988 and traveled to thirteen museums and galleries.

Since the time of his first lectures in New York and Puerto Rico (1968), Donald Jackson has had a very stimulating influence on the growth of modern Western calligraphy in the United States through the many workshops and lectures he has given. It was the first of the International Assembly of Lettering Artists seminars, inspired by Jackson, that brought him to Saint John's Abbey and University for the first time in 1981. He has since attended and lectured at several other of these annual Assemblies, including those held at Saint John's in 1984 and 1990. Jackson returned again to Saint John's in the summer of 1996 to serve as one of the keynote speakers at *Servi Textus: The Servants of the Text,* a symposium that included a calligraphy exhibition featuring Jackson's work along with that of other artists, many of whom were his past students and past associates of his atelier.

Interpretive illuminations, *incipits,* book titles, and special treatments in these volumes are the work of Donald Jackson, unless otherwise noted below.

Hazel Dolby (Illuminator — Hampshire, England)

Trained at Camberwell Art College, London, and later at the Roehampton Institute with Ann Camp, she is a Fellow of the Society of Scribes and Illuminators (FSSI). She is a lecturer at the University of Roehampton, teaching art and drawn and painted lettering, and teaches workshops in Europe and the United States. Her work is in various collections including the Poole Museum and The Crafts Study Centre, London.

Proverbs 31	Hymn to a Virtuous Woman
Zechariah 9–10	Rejoice!

Sarah Harris (Studio Manager — Abergavenny, Wales)

Attended the University of Portsmouth where she studied art, design, and media, specializing in illustration. She graduated in July 2001 and moved back to Wales, where she became assistant manager of a country hotel. Sarah joined the scriptorium team in October 2002 as a studio assistant and is now the studio manager and a contributing artist.

Wisdom 7	Correction Bee	*pulley system, with Chris Tomlin*
Song of Solomon 7–8	Butterflies	*contribution to work by Donald Jackson*

Aidan Hart (Iconographer — Shropshire, Wales)

Studied in New Zealand, the United Kingdom and Greece. He was a full-time sculptor in New Zealand before returning to the United Kingdom in 1983. Since then he has worked as a full-time iconographer. He is a member of the Orthodox Church, and his work is primarily panel icons but also includes church frescoes, illuminations on vellum, and carved work in stone and wood. His work is in collections in over fifteen countries of the world. He has contributed to numerous publications. He is visiting tutor at The Prince's School of Traditional Arts, London.

Daniel 7:1–28	Vision of the Son of Man *contribution to piece by Donald Jackson*

Thomas Ingmire (Illuminator — San Francisco, California)

Trained as a landscape architect at Ohio State University and University of California, Berkeley, before beginning the study of calligraphy and medieval painting techniques in the early '70s. He is the first foreign member to be elected (in

1977) a Fellow of the Society of Scribes and Illuminators (FSSI). Ingmire teaches throughout the United States, Canada, Australia, Europe, Japan, and Hong Kong. He has exhibited widely in the United States. His work is in many public and private collections throughout the world including the San Francisco Public Library's Special Collections, The Newberry Library, Chicago, and the Victoria and Albert Museum, London.

Job 38	Out of the Whirlwind—Where Were You
Job 40	Out of the Whirlwind—Now My Eye Sees You
Job 42	He Will Wipe Every Tear
Proverbs 1:7-8	The Fear of the Lord Is the Beginning of Knowledge
Wisdom 1:16–2:24	Let Us Lie in Wait
Isaiah 6	Messianic Predictions
Isaiah 66:3-13	As a Mother Comforts Her Child

Sally Mae Joseph (Scribe/Illuminator and Senior Artistic Consultant — Sussex, England)

Studied illumination, calligraphy, and heraldry at Reigate School of Art and Design and calligraphy, applied lettering, and bookbinding at the Roehampton Institute, London. Fellow of the Society of Scribes and Illuminators (FSSI). She has exhibited and lectured in Europe and the United States. She has contributed articles to numerous publications. She was a lecturer at Roehampton Institute 1991–1993. Her work is in many public and private collections.

Wisdom 4:7-9	But the Righteous, Though They Die
Wisdom 6:12-18	Wisdom Is Radiant—Longer
Sirach 24:19	Come to Me, You Who Desire Me
Isaiah 1:16-17	Make Yourselves Clean
Isaiah 2:4	He Shall Judge Between the Nations
Isaiah 40:1-5	Comfort, O Comfort My People
Isaiah 49:1-4	Listen to Me, O Coastlands
Isaiah 60:1-3	Arise, Shine
Jeremiah 1:4-10	Now the Word of the Lord
Micah 6:8	Do Justice, Love Kindness, Walk Humbly

Suzanne Moore (Illuminator — Vashon Island, Washington)

Earned a BFA in printmaking and drawing at the University of Wisconsin at Eau Claire, followed by the study of lettering and book design. She began creating manuscript books in the early 1980s, and melds traditional scribal techniques with contemporary aesthetics in her book work. Suzanne has taught and exhibited widely, and her books have been acquired for private and public collections in the United States and Europe, including the Pierpont Morgan Library, The Library of Congress, and The James S. Copley Library, La Jolla, California.

Sirach 24	Praise of Wisdom
Amos 4	Demands of Social Justice

Chris Tomlin (Natural History Illustrator — London, England)

Trained at the Royal College of Art, London, studying natural history illustration. He has worked for Oxford University Press and the National Trust as well as other publishers. He also studies flora and fauna in the field on expeditions as far from home as Minnesota and Madagascar, where he has worked in the rainforest recording endangered species.

Ecclesiastes	Ecclesiastes Frontispiece	*contributions to piece by Donald Jackson*
Wisdom 7	Correction Bee	*collaboration with Sarah Harris*
Isaiah 30	Scarab	
Jeremiah 17	Two Field Crickets	
Jeremiah 35	Cicada	
Ezekiel 22	Black Fly	

Diane M. von Arx (Calligrapher — Minneapolis, Minnesota)

A native Minnesotan, Diane von Arx has been a graphic designer for over thirty years, specializing in creative lettering, calligraphy, and corporate identity. She conducts workshops throughout the U.S. and Canada, and has taught in Japan and Australia. She has published three beginning calligraphy workbooks and her work has been included in numerous exhibitions and private collections. She also designed the logos for the traveling exhibitions of *The Saint John's Bible* and the titling for the documentary of the project.

Job 19:25	For I Know that My Redeemer Lives
Eccl 11:1	Send Out Your Bread upon the Waters
Sirach 6:14-22	Faithful Friends
Sirach 39:13-15	Listen

SCRIBES

In addition to writing pages throughout the book, each scribe did a text treatment in Wisdom Books and other work listed below.

Sue Hufton (London, England)

Trained at the Roehampton Institute, London, studying calligraphy and bookbinding. Fellow of the Society of Scribes and Illuminators (FSSI). Lecturer at the University of Roehampton, teaching calligraphy and bookbinding. Teaches in Europe, Canada, and Australia, and has led calligraphic retreats to Holy Island (Lindisfarne), United Kingdom. Editor of the SSI Journal *The Scribe* and has contributed articles to other publications.

Prophets and *Wisdom Books* (prose text); Sirach 24:12, 13, 15-17; English running heads

Donald Jackson (see biography above)

> *Prophets* and *Wisdom Books* (prose text and poetry text); book titles; capitals; Greek running heads

Sally Mae Joseph (see biography above)

> *Prophets* and *Wisdom Books* (poetry text); Sirach 24:19

Susan Leiper (Edinburgh, Scotland)

Born and brought up in Glasgow, Scotland. Studied French at the University of St. Andrews and History of Art at the Courtauld Institute of Art in London. After calligraphy classes in Hong Kong and Edinburgh, Susie completed the Advanced Training Scheme with the Society of Scribes and Illuminators, of which she is now a Fellow (FSSI). She has undertaken commissions for major institutions including the British Museum, The National Museums of Scotland and the BBC, and she contributed to the *Great Book of Gaelic*. She also edits books on Chinese art, which is the main source of inspiration in her own work. She lives in Edinburgh with her husband and four children.

> *Prophets* and *Wisdom Books* (prose text); Wisdom of Solomon 7:26

Brian Simpson (Leicestershire, England)

Studied calligraphy and heraldry (a fellow student of Donald Jackson) at Central School for Arts and Crafts, London, with Irene Wellington and Mervyn Oliver. Worked as a lettering artist and graphic designer for forty-nine years. Now he concentrates on calligraphy and heraldic art.

> *Prophets* and *Wisdom Books* (poetry text); all chapter numbers; capitals; Sirach 1:16

Angela Swan (Abergavenny, Wales)

Studied calligraphy and bookbinding at the Roehampton Institute from 1985 to 1988. She was an assistant to Donald Jackson in Monmouth, Wales, for three years. Angela works as a freelance calligrapher. She teaches and exhibits in the United Kingdom and has contributed to various books and publications.

> *Wisdom Books* (prose text); Wisdom of Solomon 6:12

Izzy Pludwinski (Jerusalem, Israel)

Started out as a certified religious scribe (*Sofer* STaM) and branched out to calligraphy and design. He studied at the Roehampton Institute, where he completed the certificate in Calligraphy and Design. He has taught in both London and Israel.

> All Hebrew running heads in both volumes.

OTHER TEAM MEMBERS:

> *Mabel Jackson:* Partner
> *Rebecca Cherry:* Project Manager
> *Vin Godier:* Designer and IT Consultant; computer graphics
> *Sally Sargeant:* Proofreader

Committee on Illumination and Text

Michael Patella, OSB

Michael Patella, OSB, is the chair of The Saint John's Bible Committee on Illumination and Text. He is an associate professor of New Testament and teaches in both the theology department and the School of Theology at Saint John's University, where he serves as the director of the School of Theology's Early Christian World Program. He has published in the areas of Luke, Mark, and Paul, and he also writes the "Seers' Corner" for *The Bible Today*. He earned a License in Sacred Scripture from Rome's Pontifical Biblical Institute and a doctorate in sacred scripture from the École biblique et archéologique française in Jerusalem.

Susan Wood, SCL

Susan Wood, SCL, is a professor of Theology at Marquette University, Milwaukee, Wisconsin. She taught in both the theology department and School of Theology at Saint John's University for twelve years and was the associate dean of the School of Theology for five years. She earned her bachelor's degree at Saint Mary College in Leavenworth, Kansas, her master's degree at Middlebury College, Middlebury, Vermont, and her doctorate at Marquette University, Milwaukee, Wisconsin.

Columba Stewart, OSB

Columba Stewart, OSB, is the executive director of the Hill Museum & Manuscript Library (HMML), the home of *The Saint John's Bible,* where he has developed HMML's projects of manuscript digitization in the Middle East. Having served on the CIT and as curator of special collections before becoming director of HMML, he often speaks about how *The Saint John's Bible* expresses the vision for the book arts and religious culture at Saint John's University. Father Columba has published extensively on monastic topics and is a professor of Monastic Studies at Saint John's School of Theology. He received his bachelor's degree in history and literature from Harvard College, a master's degree in religious studies from Yale University, and his doctorate in theology from the University of Oxford.

Irene Nowell, OSB

Irene Nowell, OSB, is a Benedictine from Mount St. Scholastica in Atchison, Kansas, where she is the director of junior sisters. She is an adjunct professor of Scripture for the School of Theology at Saint John's University. Sister Irene received her bachelor's degree in music from Mount St. Scholastica College in Kansas, master's degrees in German and theology from The Catholic University of America and Saint John's University. She holds a doctorate in biblical studies from The Catholic University of America.

Johanna Becker, OSB

A Benedictine potter, teacher, art historian, and Orientalist, Johanna Becker, OSB, combines these in the different facets of her work. As a teacher in the art department of the

College of Saint Benedict and Saint John's University, she taught both studio classes (primarily ceramics) and art history, focusing for the past several years on the arts of Asia. As a specialist in Asian ceramics, particularly those of seventeenth-century Japan, she has done connoisseurship for public and private museums, published a book, *Karatsu Ware*, and written and lectured worldwide. Her art history classes benefit from the years she lived in Japan and her time spent in many Asian countries as an art researcher. Sister Johanna holds a bachelor of fine arts degree from the University of Colorado, a master of fine arts degree in studio art from Ohio State University, and a doctorate in art history from the University of Michigan. Although retired, she continues to teach Asian art history classes. She is a member of the Monastery of Saint Benedict, St. Joseph, Minnesota.

Nathanael Hauser, OSB

Nathanael Hauser, OSB is an artist who works in egg tempera, enamel, calligraphy, and mosaic. While teaching art history as an associate professor at Saint John's University, he also taught calligraphy and the theology and practice of icon painting. Father Nathanael has undertaken commissions for churches, monastic communities, and private collections, creating icons, enameled crosses, calligraphy books, reliquaries, and Christmas crèches. His work and papers have been exhibited and presented in the United States and Rome, Italy. Father Nathanael received his bachelor's degree in philosophy from St. John's Seminary College in Camarillo, California. He received his bachelor's degree in sacred theology from the Pontificio Ateneo di Sant'Anselmo, Rome, and his doctorate in classical and medieval art and archaeology from the University of Minnesota.

Alan Reed, OSB

Alan Reed, OSB, is the curator of art collections at the Hill Museum & Manuscript Library. Previously Brother Alan taught design and drawing in the joint Art Department of Saint John's University and the College of St. Benedict for twenty-five years and toward the end of that time was chair of the department for six years. He has a bachelor's degree from Saint John's University in studio art, a master's of art education from the Rhode Island School of Design, and a master's of fine arts from the University of Chicago in studio art and art theory.

Ellen Joyce

Ellen Joyce teaches medieval history at Beloit College in Beloit, Wisconsin. Her research interests are in the role of visions and dreams in medieval monastic culture. She also has a passion for the study of illuminated manuscripts and their production and often teaches courses on topics related to books and their readers in the Middle Ages. She served on the CIT while she was employed at the Hill Museum & Manuscript Library and teaching at Saint John's University. Dr. Joyce received her master's and doctorate degrees from the Centre for Medieval Studies at the University of Toronto and her undergraduate degree in humanities from Yale University.

Rosanne Keller

Rosanne Keller is a sculptor whose work is on permanent display throughout the United States and the United Kingdom. In 1993 she was commissioned to create a ceramic Buddha and eight ritual vessels for the private meditation room of His Holiness, the Dalai Lama. Her sculpture can be seen at St. Deiniol's Library and St. Bueno's Jesuit Retreat Center in Wales; Saint John's University and the St. Cloud Children's Home in Minnesota; Exeter Cathedral; Taizé, France; and on the campus of Texas Woman's University. She has published a book on pilgrimage, *Pilgrim in Time*, and a novel, *A Summer All Her Own*, as well as texts for literacy programs.

Other members of the broader Saint John's community, including Susan Brix, Jerome Tupa, OSB, and David Cotter, OSB, have served at various times on the Committee for Illumination and Text.

At Saint John's University, the project is overseen by **Carol Marrin**, Director, *The Saint John's Bible*, located at the Hill Museum & Manuscript Library.

MALACHI 4

THE ART OF THE SAINT JOHN'S BIBLE